Descartes's Ballet

Other Titles of Interest from St. Augustine's Press

Zbigniew Janowski, *Augustinian-Cartesian Index*

Zbigniew Janowski, *How to Read Descartes's* Meditations

Anthony Kenny, *Descartes: A Study of His Philosophy*

Jean-Luc Marion, *Descartes's Grey Ontology: Cartesian Science and Aristotelian Thought in the* Regulae

Leszek Kolakowski, *My Correct Views on Everything*

Leszek Kolakowski, *The Two Eyes of Spinoza and Other Essays on Philosophers*

Leszek Kolakowski, *Religion: If There Is No God . . . On God, the Devil, Sin and Other Worries of the So-Called Philosophy of Religion*

Leszek Kolakowski, *Bergson*

Leszek Kolakowski, *Husserl and the Search for Certitude*

Rémi Brague, *Eccentric Culture: A Theory of Western Civilization*

Theo Verbeek, *Descartes and the Dutch: Early Reactions to Cartesian Philosophy 1637–1650*

Celia Wolf-Devine, *Descartes on Seeing: Epistemology and Visual Perception*

Gabriel Marcel, *Man against Mass Society*

Gabriel Marcel, *The Mystery of Being* (in two volumes)

Yves R. Simon, *The Great Dialogue of Nature and Space*

Stanley Rosen, *The Ancients and the Moderns: Rethinking Philosophy*

Stanley Rosen, *The Limits of Analysis*

Roger Bacon, *Roger Bacon's Philosophy of Nature: A Critical Edition, with English Translation, Introduction, and Notes, of* De multiplicatione specierum *and* De speculis comburentibus

Robert Greene, *The Death and Life of Philosophy*

Harold H. Joachim, *Descartes's Rules for the Direction of the Mind*

Josef Pieper, *Leisure, the Basis of Culture*

Josef Pieper, *Scholasticism: Personalities and Problems*

Peter Geach, *Mental Acts*

James V. Schall, S.J., *The Sum Total of Human Happiness*

Descartes's Ballet

His Doctrine of the Will and His Political Philosophy (with a transcript and English translation of La Naissance de la Paix)

Richard A. Watson

ST. AUGUSTINE'S PRESS
South Bend, Indiana
2007

Manufactured in the United States of America.

1 2 3 4 5 6   11 10 09 08 07

Library of Congress Cataloging in Publication Data
Watson, Richard A., 1931–
[Naissance de la paix. English]
Descartes's ballet: his doctrine of the will and his political
philosophy / by Richard A. Watson.
p. cm.
Includes bibliographical references and index.
ISBN 1-58731-175-5 (hardcover: alk. paper)
1. Descartes, René, 1596–1650 – Contributions in doctrine of will.
2. Will. I. Title.
B1878.W5 W3813 2003
194–dc21   2002151646

∞ The paper used in this publication meets the minimum requirements of
the American National Standard for Information Sciences – Permanence of
Paper for Printed Materials, ANSI Z39.48-1984.

ST. AUGUSTINE'S PRESS
www.staugustine.net

Contents

Preface   ix

Methodology   xiii

Chapter I. Transcript and English Translation of
La Naissance de la Paix   xvii

Chapter 2. Analysis of *La Naissance de la Paix*   28

Chapter 3. Did Descartes Write *La Naissance de la Paix*?   37

Chapter 4. Descartes's Doctrine of the Will   59

Chapter 5. Did Descartes Read Corneille?   75

Chapter 6. Descartes's Political Philosophy   86

Endnotes   115

Bibliography   121

Index   129

Monsieur,

The poem you have done me the favor of sending to me is so excellent, and contains a syllogism so ingeniously formed in the style of the School, that seeing you philosophize so well in verse, I almost find myself in a humor to want also to philosophize in verse in an attempt to respond to your courtesies. But remembering that Socrates wrote verse only when he was approaching death, for fear that this would likewise be a bad augury for me, and that one might say in Flemish that I was veygh [at the point of death], I have refrained.

– René Descartes
Letter to Constantijn Huygens, 17 February 1645
(AT IV 776–777)

PREFACE

There are two abiding mysteries in Cartesian scholarship:
1) Did Descartes write *La Naissance de la Paix?*
2) Did Descartes read Corneille?
There is no positive evidence for answering either question one way or the other. Circumstantial evidence, however, makes it virtually certain that Descartes did not write *La Naissance de la Paix* and that he did read Corneille. Nevertheless, distinguished Cartesian scholars continue to assert the contrary. And, after all –

1) Descartes could have written the verses for a ballet, and he sent a printed copy of *La Naissance de la Paix* (to weight down the packet, he said, so his accompanying letter would not be lost) to Count de Brégy. Q.E.D.

2) Descartes said he was not influenced by other thinkers, and he does not mention Corneille. Q.E.D.

These questions are interesting for two related reasons: Descartes's and Corneille's doctrines of the will are very close to one another, so it would be of value to know if either Descartes or Corneille influenced the other in the development of his views. And Descartes's doctrine of the will plays a role in any construction of his political philosophy. For such a construction, the political content of *La Naissance de la Paix* would be a valuable source – if Descartes wrote it. Also, if Descartes wrote it, *La Naissance de la Paix* would be the last of his works

published in his lifetime, and would deserve much more exten-
sive study than it has received heretofore.

In this book, I examine the evidence pertaining to all these
matters. In Chapter 1, I provide a transcript of *La Naissance de
la Paix* and the first translation of "Descartes's Ballet" into
English. In Chapter 2, I give an analysis of *La Naissance de la
Paix*. Then I argue in Chapter 3 that Hélie Poirier, a professional writer of French verse, most probably wrote the ballet. In
Chapter 4, I give an exposition of Descartes's doctrine of the
will and show how it is paralleled in Corneille. In Chapter 5, I
discuss whether Descartes read Corneille, and conclude that he
did. Finally, in Chapter 6, I construct a political philosophy
based on Descartes's writings. I show how this political philosophy is similar to that projected in *La Naissance de la Paix*,
which also embodies a doctrine of the will like Descartes's.

The official history of the ballet is as follows. On the first of
October, 1649, René Descartes – the Father of Modern
Philosophy – arrived in Stockholm as the guest of one of the
most powerful monarchs on earth, the twenty-two-year-old
Queen Christina (Descartes was fifty-three). The Queen toyed
with the great man, and is said by Adrien Baillet in his 1691
biography of Descartes to have commissioned the philosopher
to write the verses for a ballet, *La Naissance de la Paix*. Baillet
says that Descartes complied, and that Queen Christina herself
danced the role of Pallas Athena in the performance of the ballet on 9 December 1649, one day after her twenty-third birthday.
Then on 1 February 1650, in the dark of winter in a land filled,
he said, with ice and bears, where men's thoughts freeze like
the water – René Descartes caught pneumonia, and ten days
later he died.

La Naissance de la Paix consists of 344 lines of verse for a ballet written at the express command of Queen Christina on a
topic and with a political message of her setting. It celebrates
both Queen Christina's twenty-third birthday and the Peace of
Westphalia, which ended the Thirty Years' War, and which was

imposed by Swedish military might. No text of *La Naissance de la Paix* was available to Adam and Tannery when they completed their *Oeuvres de Descartes* in 1913, and in the 1974 Nouvelle Présentation of the *Oeuvres*, Pierre Costabel provides, without commentary, a text of the ballet, taken from Thibaudet and Nordström (1920), that is full of typographical errors. It has never before been translated into English. I provide a transcript and an English translation of *La Naissance de la Paix* with a discussion of its authorship. The transcript is from the 1649 French original of *La Naissance de la Paix*, printed here with the permission of the Herzog August Bibliothek, Wolfenbüttel.

No other Cartesian scholar seems to have doubted that Descartes wrote *La Naissance de la Paix*. Yet, evidence that Descartes is the author is nearly nonexistent, and there is good reason for thinking someone else wrote it. Whoever wrote it, *La Naissance de la Paix* is an important court ballet that has been much studied. And as recently as 1987, two performances were based on it, one in Stockholm and one in Los Angeles. I show just what role the ballet played in the political machinations of Christina, Queen of the Snows. And I show why I believe that Descartes did not write it.

You may indeed ask then, given that I provide an extended argument that Descartes did not write *La Naissance de la Paix*, why I think it worthwhile to publish a transcript of the verses, and more than that, translate it. There are two reasons. It does play a role in Queen Christina's development toward her abdication, and even if Descartes did not write it, there will always be Cartesian scholars who think he did.

The first draft of this study was written while I was a Fellow at the Center for Advanced Study in the Behavioral Sciences at Stanford, California. I am grateful to its Director Gardner Lindzey, and to Margaret Amara, Bruce Harley, and Deanne Dejan for their help.

I thank also librarians for assistance at the Bibliothèque Nationale in Paris, the Herzog August Bibliothek in

Wolfenbüttel, the Kungliga Biblioteket in Stockholm, the Carolina Rediviva in Uppsala, and the Washington University Library in St. Louis.

Thomas M. Lennon went over the entire manuscript, and Colette H. Winn, William H. Matheson, Maya Rybalka, Jacques Chabert, and Elyane Dezon-Jones criticized the translation in several stages, and I appreciate their care. I thank very much Susanna Åckerman, who helped me so much in Sweden, and Jean-Robert Armogathe, Jean-Marie Beyssade, Harry M. Bracken, Phillip M. Cummins, Alan Gabbey, Zbigniew Janowski, Steven Nadler, Richard H. Popkin, Emma Lewis Thomas, Susan Rosa, Britt-Marie Schiller, and Patty Jo Watson. I thank especially Lars Gustafsson of the Högskolan in Örebro whose help in this study has been invaluable. I thank Benjamin Fingerhut for his excellence in setting up this difficult text. Finally, I cannot thank too much Henry Shapiro, scholar and copy editor, master of meaning and of doggerel verse.

In my translation, I maintain the rhyme scheme but not the meter, and I have striven to retain the spirit of the original.

Some material herein has appeared in preliminary form in the *Archives de philosophie* and the *American Philosophical Association Proceedings*, and I thank their editors for permission to expand it here.

References in the text for quotations from Descartes are indicated in parentheses. AT = Adam and Tannery, eds., *Oeuvres de Descartes*. CSM = Cottingham, Stoothoff, and Murdoch, translators, *Philosophical Writings of Descartes*. Complete references are in the Bibliography. Translations not otherwise attributed are my own.

METHODOLOGY

This work consists of examples of four basic methodological procedures in doing the work of philosophy. First is *translation*, which is necessary whenever one works in a foreign language, whether the goal is publication or just essential basic comprehension. Then is *analysis*, which sometimes, as in the present case, is very like detection, in which one looks for clues, poses and treats hypotheses, searches for lost letters and hidden connections, and eventually comes to a conclusion that is usually tentative to one degree or another, as is virtually always the case in historical research. Third is *comparison* to test influences, with the case of the relationship between Descartes and Corneille being particularly pure and neat, given that not a single piece of documentary evidence exists that indicates that either man ever recognized the other's existence. Finally, there is *construction*, *not re*construction, because Descartes never constructed a political philosophy of his own, but the cutting up and rearrangement of the whole cloth of a philosopher's life and work to postulate what he would have said had he turned his mind to a task he never undertook.

These four methods are propaedeutic to the main work of historians of philosophy, the exposition and analysis of past philosophers' positions and arguments, something I have undertaken in *The Breakdown of Cartesian Metaphysics* and other writings. And what does the pursuit of history give us in the end? A good life, a lot of fun, and a glimpse into other worlds.

DESCARTES'S BALLET

Chapter 1

TRANSCRIPT AND ENGLISH TRANSLATION OF *LA NAISSANCE DE LA PAIX*

La Naissance

DE LA

PAIX
BALLET.

Dansé au chasteau Royal de Stockholm
le jour de la NAISSANCE
de sa MAJESTÉ
M DC XLIX.

IMPRIME,
Par JEAN JANSSONIUS

The Birth

OF

PEACE
BALLET.

Danced at the Royal Castle in Stockholm
on the BIRTHDAY
of her MAJESTY
M DC XLIX.

PRINTED,
By JEAN JANSSONIUS

RECIT. Chanté avant le BALLET.

QU'ON observe icy le silence,
　　Et qu'on revere la presence
De la divinité qui preside en ces lieux,
Elle nous veut tirer des perils de la guerre,
　　Et malgré plusieurs autres Dieux,　　　　5
Elle veut que la Paix reviene sur la Terre.

　　Reconnoissons que cete Paix
　　Est le plusgrand de ses bienfaits.

　　Jusques icy par sa prudence
　　Et par la secrete influence,　　　　10
Des ordres genereux qu'elle nous a donnez
Nous avons combatu avec tant d'avantage.
　　Que de grans peuples estonnez
Ont pris la loy de nous & nous rendent homage.
　　Mais la Naissance de la Paix　　　　15
　　Est le plusgrand de ses bienfais.

Celebrons donc cette Naissance,
　　Et remarquons en cete Danse,
Ou la guerre & la Paix estalent leur pouvoir,
Que Pallas a raison de penser que la guerre,　　20
　　La meilleure qu'on puisse avoir,
Oste tousjours beaucoup des beautez de la terre,
　　Et que de nous donner la Paix
　　C'est le plusgrand de ses bienfais.

LES VERS DU BALLET. De la Naissance de la Paix.
Pour MARS *qui danse la Premiere Entrée.*

IE veux faire trembler tous les coins de la Terre,　　25
Et monstrer aux mortels qu'aucun des autres Dieux

SOLO Sung before the BALLET.

LET US observe here the silence,
 And revere the presence
Of the divinity who presides over these premises.
She wishes to draw us from the perils of war,
 And, despite several other gods' pleas,   5
She desires peace on Earth to restore.

 Let us recognize of this Peace that it's
 The greatest of all her benefits.

 Until now by her prudence
 And by the secret influence   10
Of the generous orders she has propounded,
We have fought with so much advantage
 That mighty nations, astounded,
Have adopted our laws and render us homage.
 But the Birth of Peace, everyone admits, 15
 Is the greatest of all her benefits.

Celebrate, therefore, this Birthing
 And observe in this Dancing,
Where war and Peace display their power,
That Pallas is right to think that war,   20
 Even in its finest possible flower,
Is always of earth's beauties a grim reaper,
 And that to give us Peace as, everyone admits,
 Is the greatest of all her benefits.

THE VERSE OF THE BALLET. Of the Birth of Peace.
For MARS *who dances the First Dance.*

I intend to make all earth's corners quake, 25
And to demonstrate to mortals that no other god

N'eut jamais tant que moy de pouvoir en ces lieux.
Non pas mesme celuy qui lance le tonerre.
    Ses esclairs & ses feux ne font qu'un peu de peur,
Au lieu que mes canons & mes autres machines,   30
Mes mortiers, mes petards, mes brusleaux & mes mines
Portent partout la mort avecque la terreur.

    J'ecrose les rochers, j'applanis les montagnes,
Je comble les fossez, je mine les chasteaux,
J'ensanglante les mers, je brusle les vaisseaux   35
Et je jonche de morts les plus belles campagnes.

Pour quatre gros, deux de Cavalerie & deux d'Infantrie, qui
representent un cors d'Armeé conduit par PALLAS, *en la*
Seconde Entrée

MARS ne doit pas s'attribuer
Le premier honneur de la guerre,
Encor qu'il puisse remüer
Le Ciel, la Mer, l'Air & la Terre.   40
C'est la Fille de Jupiter
Qui seule peut le meriter.

C'est PALLAS de qui la prudence
Est si bien jointe a la valeur,
Que jamais le trop d'assurance   45
Ne luy donne trop de chaleur.
Elle est sage, elle est vigilante,
Elle est courageuse, & constante.

    Aussy est elle en nostre corps
Le chef sans quoy il ne peut vivre;   50
Et nous faisons tous nos efforts
Pour avoir l'honneur de la suivre.
Sans elle ce cors divisé
Seroit d'un chascun mesprisé.

Ever had as much power as I do on this sod,
Not even he who casts thunderbolts in his wake.
   His lightning bursts and fires cause only petty fear,
Whereas my cannons and other machines,   30
My mortars, bombs, firebrands, and mines,
Bring death with terror everywhere.

   I crush boulders, I flatten mountains,
I bridge moats, I undermine castles,
I bloody seas, I burn vessels,   35
And I strew the dead on the most beautiful plains.

For four fat fellows, two from the Cavalry and two from the
Infantry who represent an Army corps, commanded by PALLAS
in the Second Dance.

MARS ought not himself make
The most honored in war.
For even if he can shake
The Heavens, the Earth, the Sea, and the Air,   40
It is Jupiter's Daughter
Alone who merits the honor.

In PALLAS prudence
Is so well joined with valor
That never has excessive confidence
Excited in her excessive ardor.   45
She is wise, she is vigilant,
She is courageous and constant.

   She is therefore in our corps
The head without which it could not stir.   50
And we exert all our efforts
To have the honor of following her.
Without her this body divided
Would be by all despised.

Pendant qu'il luy plaist nous conduire   55
Tous les païs nous sont ouvers,
Rien est capable de nous nuire
Nous pouvons vaincre l'univers.
Et nous avons souvent la Gloire
D'amener icy la Victoire.   60

Pour la Terreur Panique qui danse la Troisiesme Entrée.

C'EST a tort que PALLAS & MARS
Se vantent que dans les hasars
Leur pouvoir est incomparable,
Le mien est bien plus redoutable.
Il leur faut beaucoup de travail: 65
Il leur faut un grand attirail:
De poudres, de chevaux & d'armes,
Et de gens qui vont aux alarmes,
Pour ne livrer qu'un seul combat
Ou assez souvent on les bat,   70
Encor qu'ilz facent bonne mine
Et qu'ils soient de race divine.

Mais moy qui fais bien moins de bruit,
Moy qui suis fille de la nuit,
Qui suis froide, pale & tremblante,   75
Quand je veux donner l'espouvante
A un milion de guerriers,
Et fouler aux pieds leurs lauriers,
Il ne me faut qu'une chimere,
Un songe, ou une ombre legere,   80
Qui j'envoye dans leurs cerveaux.
Et ils tremblent comme des veaux
Ils fuient, ils devienent blesmes,
Et souvent se jetent eux mesmes,
En des maux plus a redouter   85
Que ceux quilz pensent eviter.

As long as it pleases her to lead us,   55
All lands are open to our traverse.
Nothing then can harm us,
We can vanquish the universe.
And we often have the Glory
Of bringing home Victory.   60

For Panic Terror who dances the Third Dance.

IT IS wrong for PALLAS and MARS
To brag that in risky ventures
Their power is incomparable,
For mine is much more formidable.
For them, much work is necessary   65
And much equipment they must carry:
Powder, horses, and arms,
And soldiers to answer alarms,
To rally for just one fight,
Where very often they're put to flight,   70
Even though they put on a good face
And are of a godly race.

But I, who am so much more quiet,
I, who am the daughter of the night,
Cold, pale, and trembling here,   75
When I want to give men fear,
Into a million soldiers terror put,
And trample all their laurels underfoot,
A chimera is all I need,
A dream, mere shadow of a deed,   80
That I send into their brains.
Then they tremble like calves with pains,
They flee, turn white,
And often fling themselves quite,
Onto evils of which they should be more afraid   85
Than those they are trying to evade.

Pour quelques fuyarts que la Terreur Panique a fait sortir de
l'Armée avant le combat en la Quatuorsiesme Entrée.

AUX DAMES.

NOUS nous sommes bien defendus.
    Mais nous estions vendus.
Tous nos chefs n'ont rien fait qui vaille.
      Tous les chams sont couverts de cors.   90
         Tous les nostres sont morts.
Nous avons perdu la bataille.

    Les ennemis sont icy pres.
      Nous accourons expres.
Affin d'estre vostre defense   95
    S'ils vienent nous leur ferons voir,
      Que nous avons pouvoir
De punir leur outrecuidance.

    Cheres beautez n'ayez pas peur
      Que nous manquions de coeur,   100
Bienque vous reteniez les nostres,
    Nous serons assez valeureux,
      Et aussy tresheureux.
S'il vous plaist nous donner les vostres.

Pour les Volontaires qui se rendent au camp lors qu'on se
prepare a donner bataille & dansent la Cinquiesme Entrée.

    Nous allons courageusement,   105
Sans craindre le fer, ny la flamme,
Pour ayder a l'enlevement
D'une tresbelle & riche Dame.
Et nous n'y cherchons que des coups,
Car la Dame n'est pas pour nous.   110

For some fugitives whom Panic Terror has made flee the Army
before combat in the Fourth Dance.

TO THE LADIES.

Our defense was mighty stout.
　　But we have been sold out.
Our commanders accomplish only fiddle-faddle.
　　All the fields are covered with bodies bled.　　90
　　　　All our comrades now are dead.
We have lost the battle.

　　The enemy is very close.
　　　　We rushed here for one purpose,
Which is to be your defense.　　95
　　　　If they come, we'll make them see
　　　　　　That we have the power, we,
To punish their presumptuous offense.

　　Have no fear, beauties dear,
　　　　That our hearts are lacking here,　　100
Even though you have ours.
　　　　We still retain sufficient heart,
　　　　　　And will be happy for our part,
If you would please now give us yours.

For the Volunteers who come to the camp while everyone is
preparing to give battle and dance the Fifth Dance.

　　We advance in courageous production,　　105
Without fear of sword or of flame,
To aid in the abduction
Of a very beautiful and rich Dame.
But we'll get only blows and fuss,
For the Lady herself is not for us.　　110

Le plus haut point de nostre attente,
C'est qu'affin de nous resiouir
Peut estre nous pourrons jouir
De sa Demoyselle suivante.
Pour tel prix nous ne craignons pas,   115
De nous exposer au trepas.

    Si vous doutiez de nos courages
Vous pourriez oyant ce dessein
Penser que nous sommes peu sages,
Et que nostre esprit est mal sain.   120
Et peut estre aussy que nos belles
Nous estimeroient infidelles.

Mais quand nous vous aurrons appris
Quelle est cete fille suivante
Dont chascun de nous se contente,   125
Vous cesserez d'estre surpris.
Car cete suivante est la Gloire
Et sa Maitresse est la Victoire.

Pour la Victoire qui danse la sixiesme Entrée.

ENcor que cete cour soit remplie de Dames
    Qu'on ne peut trop estimer,   130
      Et que les plus nobles ames
        Sont obligées d'aymer.
Je surpasse pourtant en beauté les plus belles.
    Et ce qui en fait foy,
C'est que pour un amant qui souspire pour elles   135
    Mille meurent pour moy.

Pour des soldats estropiez qui dansent la Septiesme Entrée.

QUi voit comme nous sommes faits
Et pense que la guerre est belle,

The highest level of our expectation,
Is that to attain our happiness:
We may manage to possess
The lady's-maid in her delegation.
We have no fear, for such a prize,　　　115
To put in jeopardy our lives.

　　If you doubt our courage,
You might, having heard of our plan of attack,
Think we're not so sage,
And our characters out of whack.　　　120
And perhaps also that our own beauties
Will think us unfaithful to our duties.

　　But when you comprehend
The identity of the lady's-maid here implied,
With whom each of us is satisfied,　　　125
Your surprise will end,
Because this lady's-maid is Glory,
And her mistress is Victory.

For Victory who dances the Sixth Dance.

EVEN though this court is filled with Ladies
　　That no one could esteem too much,　　　130
　　And that the most noble souls with great ease
　　　Must love, adore, and such,
Yet I am lovlier than the lovliest of these.
　　And what proves this completely
Is that for every lover who sighs for them, if you please 135
　　A thousand die for me.

For some crippled soldiers who dance the Seventh Dance.

WHO sees how we have been undone
Yet praises war in beauty's name,

Ou qu'elle vaut mieux que la Paix,
Est estropié de ceruelle.   140

Pour des Gouiats qui vont au pillage & dansent la
Huictiesme Entrée.

NOstre fortune est estimée
La plusheureuse de l'armee,
Car nous n'allons jamais aux coups,
Nos maistres combatent pour nous.
Et quand ils ont de l'avantage   145
Nous allons mieux qu'eux au pillage.
Mais quel butin que nous facions,
Quel profit que nous en tirions.
Nous ne devenons jamais riches,
Car nous ne scaurions estre chiches.   150
Nous dissipons sans jugement
Ce que nous gaignons promptement.
Estant un jour en l'abondance,
Et l'autre faisant penitence.
Nous avons tant de mauvais temps,   155
Et nous sommes si peu contens,
Qu'il faut avoüer que personne
Ne peut trouver la guerre bonne;
Que tous ses fruits sont tresmauvais:
Et qu'on doit desirer la Paix.   160
Car nostre vie est estimée
La plushureuse de l'armée.

Pour des Paysans ruinez qui dansent la neufiesme Entrée

NOus pouvons assez assurer,
Sans avoir besoin de jurer,
Que la guerre nous est nuisible.   165
Mais on a sujet de penser
Que nostre coeur est peu sensible
Lors qu'on nous voit icy danser.

Thinks Peace in worth the lesser one,
Is crippled badly in his brain.   140

For some Camp Followers who come to pillage and dance the
Eighth Dance.

IT's estimated that our lot
Is the happiest the Army's got,
Because we never enter in a fight.
Our masters combat for our delight.
And when they win and earn the day,   145
We pillage better than even they.
But whatever booty that we take,
Whatever profit from it make,
We never ever rich become,
Because we don't know how to save the sum.   150
We squander without reasonable aim
Promptly all the plunder that we gain.
We live one day in abundance,
The next we spend in penitence.
The times that come are bad so often,   155
And contentment's seldom there to soften,
That we don't see how anyone could
Find war and battles to the good.
The fruits of war are muck and mire,
So Peace is what one should desire,   160
Because it's estimated that our lot
Is the happiest the Army's got.

For some ruined Peasants who dance the Ninth Dance.

WE can well enough guarantee,
With no need of oaths to back our plea,
That war brings on us a great blight.   165
But people are inclined to think
That we are not very bright
When they see us dancing on its brink.

Toutefois si on considere
Qu'estans en extreme misere   170
Nous n'avons ny chevaux ny boeufs
Pour travailler a nostre ouvrage;
Ny beurre ny poules, ny oeufs
Pour porter vendre hors du vilage.

On connoist que la pauvreté   175
Nous enseigne l'oisiveté.
Et que n'ayant plus rien a craindre,
Nous n'avons plus aussy besoin
D'employer du tems a nous plaindre
C'est pourquoy nous sommes sans soin.   180

Pour la Terre qui danse avec les trois autres elemens en la
Dixiesme Entrée.

VOYANT le feu parmy les eaux,
Lors qu'il y brusle des vaisseaux:
Et le sentant en ma poitrine,
Lors qu'enfermé dans une mine
Il me dechire, & fait voler   185
Plusieurs de mes membres en l'air:
Voyant cet air rempli de poudre,
Et de feux pires que la foudre:
Enfin voyant que les combats
Troublent tous les corps d'icy bas.   190
Je crains qu'en peu de tems le monde
Ne perisse ou ne se confonde,
Et face un chaos, si les Dieux
N'envoyent la Paix en ces lieux.

Recit chanté dans le ciel avant l'Vnziesme Entrée, ou
PALLAS *danse seule.*

BIENQUE la guerre vous outrage   195

Nevertheless, if one comprehends
What being in extreme poverty portends: 170
Horses and cattle have we none
To make our daily round,
No butter, no chickens, no eggs, not one
To take to sell outside the town.

Everyone knows that poverty   175
Teaches one to be lazy,
And that having nothing left to fear,
We can no longer bear
To spend our time complaining here,
Which explains why we live without care.   180

For Earth who dances with the three other elements in the
Tenth Dance.

SEEING fire among the waters burning,
When it consumes vessels there churning,
And feeling it in my chest,
When in a mine it is compressed,
It rends me, and makes fly   185
Several of my limbs into the sky.
Seeing powder filling the air,
And fires worse than thunder-bolts there,
Finally seeing that the fight
Disturbs all bodies here below in sight,   190
I fear that soon the world so tossed
Will either perish or be lost,
And face a chaos, if divinity
Does not settle Peace upon this vicinity.

Solo sung in the heavens before the Eleventh Dance, which
PALLAS dances alone.

THOUGH war fills you with outrage,   195

Et que MARS semble s'obstiner
A vous vouloir tous ruiner,
Peuples, ne perdez point courage.
   PALLAS a pouvoir du destin
   D'y metre bientost une fin.   200

   Les victoires luy sont certaines
Lors qu'il luy plaist de les chercher.
Mais vostre bien luy est plus cher.
Elle est lasse de voir vos peines.
   Et elle a pouvoir du destin   205
   D'y metre bientost une fin.

   Remerciez donc sa clemence
Des bons desseins qu'elle a conceus
Et pour les maux desia receus
Souffrez les avec patience: 210
   Car elle a pouvoir du destin
   D'y metre bientost une fin.

Pour la Iustice qui danse avec Pallas & Paix en la
Douxiesme Entree.

PALLAS m'ordonne tousjours
D'accompagner ses armées,
Pour ce que sans mon secours,   215
Elles seroient trop blasmées.

   Mais elle m'ordonne aussy
D'estre compagne fidelle
De la Paix, qui vient icy
Pour y regner avec elle.   220

   Et j'espere desormais
Pouvoir estre si constante

And MARS seems in his obstination
To want to lead you all into ruination,
Earth's peoples, do not lose courage.
    Pallas has power from destiny,
    Soon to end the infamy.   200

    Her victories are certain
When seeking them pleases her,
But to her, your well-being is more dear.
She's tired of seeing your pain.
    And she has power from destiny,   205
    Soon to end the infamy.

    Thank her for her clemency,
The good designs she has conceived,
And as for the wrongs you have received,
Suffer them patiently,   210
    Because she has power from destiny,
    Soon to end the infamy.

For Justice who dances with Pallas and Peace in the
Twelfth Dance.

PALLAS always orders me
To accompany her armies at their game,
For unless I oversee,   215
They would reap excessive blame.

    But she also gives me orders
To be a true companion dear
Of Peace, now within our borders,
To rule with her here.   220

    And I hope in the future
To be so steadfast

A maintenir cete Paix
Qu'elle fera florissante.

Pour tous les Dieux qui deliberent de la Paix en la
Treziesme Entree.

NOs interests sont si divers,   225
Que nous ne sommes pas a croire
En ce qui regarde la gloire
Et le biens de tout l'univers.

    Car MARS, par exemple, seroit
Blasmable, s'il n'aymoit la guerre,   230
Et au contraire si la Terre
L'aymoit, ou s'en estonneroit.

    PALLAS seule est egalement
Et belliqueuse, & pacifique,
Qu'aucun de nous donc ne se pique   235
De controler son jugement.

Pour Mercure, a la Renommée qui danse avec luy lors qu'il vient
publier la Paix en la Quatorsiesme Entrée.

DEMEURE apres moy Renommée.
Car tu es si accoustumée
A mentir quand tu vais devant,
Que les plus sages bien souvant   240
Ne jugent vray que le contraire
De ce que tu veux faire croire.

Response pour la Renommée.

    Es tu donc plus que moy croyable?
Es tu moins que moy reprochable?

This peace to nurture
That it will flourish and last.

*For all the Gods who deliberate about Peace in the
Thirteenth Dance.*

OUr interests are so diverse   225
That we are not to be believed
When glory's to be received,
And the goods of all the universe.

   Because MARS, for example, would become
Blamable if he did not love war,   230
While to the contrary, if Earth were
To love it, this would astonish everyone.

   PALLAS alone is one and the same,
On peace and war best.
Therefore, none of us should dare to claim   235
To check or control her judgement.

*For Mercury, to Fame who dances with him when he comes to
proclaim the Peace in the Fourteenth Dance.*

STAY behind me, Fame.
Because you are so accustomed in your name
To lie when you are in the lead,
That the wisest sages often need   240
To judge the reverse as true,
Of what is claimed by you.

Response by Fame.

   You're more credible than me?
You're less reproachable than me?

Toy qui es le Dieu des marchans,   245
Et des larrons les plus mechans;
Toy de qui les maquerelages
Ont escroqué mains pucelages.
Mais quand tu annonce la Paix
Puisse tu ne mentir jamais.   250

Pour Apollon qui danse avec Pallas en la Quinziesme Entrée.

MAINTENANT que la Paix est faite,
Et que MARS a fait sa retraite,
PALLAS se peut servir de moy,
Pour reparer en peu d'années
Toutes les places ruinées   255
Des estatz soumis a sa loy.

   Et j'ay de tresbonnes raisons
Pour assurer que mes chansons
Ne luy seront pas inutiles.
Car comme Amphion autrefois,   260
Par les seuls accors de ma voix
J'ay pouvoir de bastir des viles.

Pour les neuf Muses qui dansent la Seziesme Entrée.

NOus venons pour inviter
Les Dames a imiter
Leur trescavante Maitresse,   265
PALLAS qui n'ignore rien,
Et dont le souverain bien
Est d'avoir de la sagesse.

   S'il leur plaist apercevoir
Quel est nostre grand scavoir,   270
Et de quel sexe nous sommes:

You, the god of common tradesmen,   245
And of the most wicked highwaymen;
You, whose pimps in sordid beds
Have stolen many maidenheads.
But when you announce the coming of Peace,
May all your lies forever cease.   250

For Apollo who dances with Pallas in the Fifteenth Dance.

NOW that Peace is made complete,
And MARS has taken his retreat,
PALLAS can use my aid,
In a very few years to repair
And in very few years repair   255
In states where her law is now obeyed.

   And my reasons are very good
For thinking that my singing would
Be done here not in vain.
Because, as once did Amphion,   260
By the mere sound of my voice in song
I build towns where rubble's lain.

For the nine Muses who dance the Sixteenth Dance.

WE have come to invite
The ladies to imitate
Their Mistress, the very wise,   265
PALLAS, who is ignorant of nothing,
And for whom the sovereign good thing
In having wisdom lies.

   If they would please pay attention
To our great scope of comprehension,   270
And of which sex we are a part,

Elles ne pourront ceder
La gloire de posseder
Tous les arts a aucuns hommes.

    Mesme si elles n'ont soin   275
De les passer de bien loin,
Elles n'auront point d'excuses:
D'autant que nous nous trouvons
Dans le lieu ou nous vivons,
Pour un Apollon, neuf Muses.   280

Pour la Terre qui danse avec les trois Graces en la
Dix-septiesme Entrée.

NE vous estonnez pas de me voir jeune & belle,
Moi qui vous paroissois tantost tout autrement:
Mon naturel est tel que je me renouvelle
Si tost que je jouis de mon contentement.

Quand mes bois sont coupez, mes viles ruinées,   285
Tous mes chams delaissez, mes chasteaux demolis:
On peut dire a bon droit que j'ay maintes années,
Et que mes membres morts sont presque ensevelis.

    Mais la Paix revenant on repare mes viles,
On seme d'autres bois, on fait d'autres chasteaux,   290
On cultive mes chams pour les rendre fertiles,
Et j'ay par ce moyen des membres tous nouveaux.

Pour Ianus qui ferme les portes de son temple en la
dix-huitiesme Entree.

VOus ne devez estre estonnez
De me voir avec deux visages.
Je suis mis au nombre des sages   295
Par ceux qui me les ont donnez.

Then women will never yield
The Glory of possessing any field
To any men in any art.

    Even if they have no care 275
To much surpass men everywhere,
They will have no excuses,
Because we find there is,
Where each of us now lives,
For one Apollo, nine Muses. 280

          For Earth who dances with the three Graces in the
                    Seventeenth Dance.

DON'T be astonished to see my beauty and youth,
I who just now appeared to you so different;
To renew myself is my nature in truth,
So quickly that I frolic in content.

When my woods are cut and my towns gone to seed, 285
My fields abandoned, my castles demolished,
One could rightly say that I am ancient indeed,
And that my dead limbs are nearly abolished.

    But Peace returned, everyone repairs my villages.
Everyone plants woods and builds castles, new scenes. 290
They make my fields into fertile tillages.
And I have all new members by these means.

          For Janus who closes the doors of his temple in the
                  Eighteenth Dance.

YOu should not astonished be
To see me in this guise,
For I am numbered among the wise, 295
By those who gave two faces to me.

Ils ont creu que le souvenir
Des choses qui ont cessé d'estre
Servoit a me faire connoistre
Les choses qui sunt a venir. 300

Et j'ay deux fronts pour ce sujet.
L'un est derriere, & represente
Toute la vie precedente,
L'autre a l'avenir pour object.

Or on a creu communement 305
Que ces deux fronts estoient semblables,
Mais les tems estant variables
On en doit juger autrement.

Ainsy n'ayant jusques icy
Rien vu qu'une treslongue guerre, 310
Et la Paix venant sur la Terre
Pour nous delivrer de souci.

On croira, sans estre scavant,
Ny rien penser d'extrordinaire,
La visage que j'ay derriere 315
Moins beau que celuy de devant.

Pour les Cavaliers qui dansent UN GRAND BALLET En la
DIX-NEUFIESME ENTREE, A PALLAS.

ADORABLE PALLAS dont le divin pouvoir
Preside egalement a tous les exercices
Et de guerre, & de Paix, qui repugnent aux vices,
Qui pourroit vous suivant manquer a son devoir? 320

Nous qui avons l'honneur d'estre vos chevaliers,
Nous desirons vous suivre, aussy bien sur Parnasse,

They think that memory,
Of what has ceased to be,
Served to make me see
Things that are to come to be.   300

And I have two faces for these reasons:
The one behind shows as receding
All of life that was preceding;
The other's object is future seasons.

Now people have commonly thought   305
That these two faces are comparable.
But because the times are variable,
To judge otherwise people ought.

Having until now, thus,
Seen nothing but a very long war,   310
With peace coming to Earth's shore,
From care to deliver us.

You'll agree, without being a bred,
That it's not extraordinary to find
The face I have behind   315
Less lovely than the one ahead.

For the Cavaliers who dance A GRAND BALLET In the
NINETEENTH DANCE, TO PALLAS.

Most holy PALLAS, whose divine might
Presides equally over every exercise,
Whether of war or of Peace, who loathes vice,
Who, following you, could not do right?   320

We who are honored to be your knights, who
Desire to follow you, not only on the heights of Parnassus,

Que dans les chams poudreux du puissant Dieu de Thrace,
Pour paroistre avec vous, & ceuillir des lauriers.

    Mais nous n'esperons pas aller si haut que vous, 325
Ce mont a des degrés: plus un chascun en passe,
Plus on juge qu'il a de scavoir & de grace:
Vous seule avez monté sur le plushaut de tous.

    Et cela nous suffit, nous vivons dans un corps,
Dont nous sommes les bras, vous la divine flamme   330
Qui seule conduit tout, & qu'on appele l'ame.
C'est assez pour les bras qu'ils soient souples & forts.

    RECIT Chanté avant le GRAND BALLET des DAMES ou
PALLAS la Paix & la justice dansent avec les MUSES & les
Graces.

PEuples que pensez vous voyant tant de merueilles,
Qui vous eblouissent les yeux?
On n'en a jamais vû sur terre des pareilles.   335
Pensez que vostre esprit est ravi dans les cieux.

    Vous allez voir Pallas, les Muses, & les Graces,
      La justice, & la Paix aussy.
Ne jugerez vous pas, en regardant leurs faces,
Que tout, ce qui est beau dans le ciel, est icy?   340

    Par PALLAS on entend la sagesse eternelle;
      C'est PALLAS qui regne en ce lieu.
La justice & la Paix y regnent avec elle.
Et pourtant nous n'avons qu'une Reine, & un Dieu.

FIN.

But also in the gunpowdered fields of the powerful god of Thrace,
To gather up laurels by appearing with you.

But to go as high as you is beyond our hope.   325
This mountain has degrees: the more one climbs to a higher place,
The more we judge him wise and full of grace:
You alone have climbed the very highest slope.

It is enough for us; in a body we belong
Of which we are the arms. You are the divine flame we call the soul, 330
Which alone commands the whole game.
It is enough for the arms, to be supple and strong.

SOLO. Sung before the GRAND BALLET of LADIES in which
PALLAS, Peace, and justice dance with the MUSES and the
Graces.

People, what do you think, seeing so many splenders
That dazzle your eyes?
Nothing ever seen on earth engenders.   335
Such thoughts that transport your spirit to the skies.

Now you will see PALLAS, the Muses, and the Graces,
Justice and Peace, do not fear.
Will you not think, seeing their faces,
That all that is beautiful in heaven is here?   340

By Pallas, we meant eternal wisdom; to be plain,
PALLAS rules here.
Justice and Peace with her reign,
Yet we have but one Queen and one god.

THE END

Chapter 2

ANALYSIS OF
LA NAISSANCE DE LA PAIX

Descartes's presence in the court of Queen Chrisina, the Lion of the North, at a time when the philosopher was seeking respite from the attacks of Protestant ministers in The Netherlands is circumstantial evidence that he approved of monarchy for the imposition of order. (In 1647 and 1648, he had visited France in the same quest, where he had been offered a pension – never paid – by Mazarin.) He approved of the state-imposed peace, and I take it that he also approved of the victors enjoying the spoils of war and annexing territory, because Queen Christina is said to have promised to give him a castle in Pomerania, a province that only lately had been a part of Germany.

As discussed below, court ballets were often vehicles of political propaganda. Queen Christina almost certainly dictated the ideas in the set of five ballets of which *La Naissance de la Paix* is the third, because they fit exactly into her Byzantine political maneuvering in the Swedish court. The question here is whether or not the doctrine of the will and the political philosophy expressed in *La Naissance de la Paix* are Cartesian. If so, this provides a kind of internal evidence for the claim that Descartes wrote the ballet. Let us proceed verse by verse to see.

Solo Sung before the Ballet

The presiding divinity who yearns to withdraw us from the perils of war is Queen Christina, in the guise of Pallas Athena, the goddess of peace, who despite the pleas of Mars, the god of war, intends to restore peace. In the political context of the Thirty Years' War, this is to place Sweden in the role of peacemaker, wiser than the other nations and their leaders. The role of a strong state and a wise leader, then, is to impose and maintain peace over lesser nations and less-wise leaders. The greatest benefit a wise ruler and state can provide is peace.

Sweden did fight fiercely, and did astound the other nations. The Lion of the North also reaped great spoils of war, and annexed much territory including Pomerania. Even after she abdicated on 6 July 1654 in favor of her cousin Karl Gustav (something she imposed with great power of will in opposition to the desires of her advisers that she marry Karl and bear an heir), Christina continued to receive a major portion of her income from Pomerania. Had Descartes lived, Queen Christina would very likely have given him a pension and a castle in Pomerania.

Throughout the ballet, there is disapproval of the destruction and disruption of war, but no disdain for the wealth and the power that come from winning.

First Dance

Mars claims to be the greatest of all gods because he can cause so much destruction. He points out that Jupiter has nothing but thunderbolts, but the god of war now has derived great advantages from the advancement of modern science and technology. Cannons, mortars, bombs, all the possibilities of gunpowder are employed. There are also the machines of war, to pound, dig, and blast. And the point is sharp. The purpose of this armory is to spread terror and death, to seed the meadows with dead soldiers.

Second Dance

Four roughnecks, two from the Cavalry and two from the infantry represent an army corps commanded by Pallas. They argue that despite Mars's power, Pallas is greater than he, for her actions are guided by wisdom. In the Cartesian mode, she understands her own abilities and is not overconfident. She proceeds with her passions in control, she watches carefully, she is gentlemanly (as Mars is not), and finally – a most important Cartesian virtue – her will is steadfast and firm.

Pallas is the head of the army, a head that soldiers gladly follow by acting as her limbs. The body should follow reason. Such a leader is necessary to avoid chaos, and Descartes certainly believed that this principle of one person in charge held all the way to the monarchy. Intelligent soldiers and citizens desire to follow a noble leader to share in her honor. And when we all work in unity following the sovereign, nothing can impede advance. The universe is at the wise and constant leader's feet.

Third Dance

These are perhaps the ballet's most successful verses, and they are very Cartesian. Great wisdom and great will power as represented by Pallas and Mars are all very well, but both can be riddled from below. Like rats tunneling into a granary, the bodily passions can destroy the best intentions of the wisest and strongest men. Panic terror makes gibbering idiots of soldiers. They abandon all their arms and flee. But it is all in their heads. Not that the danger is not real, but their response is not to objective danger, but to subjective fear. Terror invades their brains, and makes them tremble like terrified calves, and this in turn makes them desire to flee. And when they do, they get into worse trouble than before. The Cartesian moral is evident: the passions must be controlled.

Fourth Dance

The fugitives who fled in terror now must try to redeem themselves. They claim in a refrain as old as armies that their commanders sold them out. The underlying point here is that generals, not soldiers, win and lose battles. Both Queen Christina and Descartes certainly believed that a strong commander can provide the example and instruction that lead soldiers to over-come panic.

In fact, the fugitives say to the ladies of the court to whom they have fled, they have retreated to protect the women. But the text suggests that they may expect something in return for their services.

Fifth Dance

Never fear, the volunteers are arriving to save the day. Look, they are very brave, with great derring-do, but they apparently are going to kidnap one of the ladies of the court. Yet they say she is safe. All they want for rescuing her – for that is what they are doing – are some kisses from her chambermaids. So what do we have here? It seems to be a batch of volunteers rushing in and grabbing the maids, retreating from battle to engage in dalliance. What will we think about their good sense? What will their wives think?

What did Queen Christina think? She loved it. Queen Christina was oddly sexed. She was raised like a prince. and it has been suggested that she was a lesbian, or even a hermaph-rodite. Whether she was either, her behavior was like that of a pre-pubescent child who delights in teasing adults. She loved to embarrass people with sexual innuendo, and on one occasion she taught her maids in waiting (who supposedly did not know French) a litany of dirty French songs that she had them sing in the presence of M. de la Thuillerie, the old and dignified French Ambassador to Sweden.[1] So the mime dancing that went with the verses was doubtless ribald.

But then the risqué implications are banished, for it turns out that the lady the volunteers are whisking away is Victory, and the chambermaid they are most interested in getting their hands on is Glory. (Consistency is not at premium here, as the cowards gather up Victory and gain Glory.)

Sixth Dance

Victory, then, is sweet, the greatest beauty of all. And the sexual implications return, with a vicious sting. For every conquest made by your ordinary belle, a thousand men die seeking Glory in Victory's name.

Seventh Dance

While Panic Terror's verses are the greatest for verve and bounce, those for the crippled soldiers are the bluntest. War is hell. Anybody who romanticizes it is crippled in his brain. It is certainly Cartesian to pinpoint the problem in the brain, not in the soul. The soul is pure; it is the brain that needs conditioning. Reason will convince everyone that peace is better than war; it is only the inability of some to overcome their bodily passions that leads to war.

Eighth Dance

Camp followers would seem to have a good life. The soldiers fight for them, and they just come along behind to loot and pillage. Their problem is that they do not have good sense, so they waste all their plunder. Their lives, then, are totally inconstant. One day they have more than enough; the next day they have nothing. It is their weakness of will that makes them so pitiful and despicable.

These verses do not indicate that the spoils of war are in themselves bad, but that war is bad to the extent that it gives opportunity to looters such as these camp followers. They cannot restrain their bodily desires, and so live pendulum lives of feast and famine. War demoralizes by generating the conditions for inconstancy.

Ninth Dance

The disruption of war is shown further by the ruined peasants, who are dancing on the debris of their very livelihood. How could they be so gay when their horses and cattle are gone, they have nothing to eat, and there is not even a single egg to sell? The answer is that losing everything and descending into total poverty is completely demoralizing. They have nothing more to lose, but also there would seem to be – in the midst of war – no reason to strive to do anything at all. Theirs is a dance of despair.

Tenth Dance

Whoever wrote the ballet had a flair for verses of chaos and destruction. Earth, air, fire, and water engage in a wild dance of disruption as war – and above all, the incendiary forces of gunpowder – blasts and ignites all the elements, tossing everything into the air in a wild and frightful chaos. The scene is one of hell on earth. The only hope is that the gods will bring peace. In the midst of this chaos, the scene changes for the second act.

Solo Sung before the Eleventh Dance

Now Pallas appears to reassure everyone that no matter how desperate things look, she – her power of reason over the passions – assures victory. She is reluctant to go to war against the destructive forces of Mars, but she wants to bring peace to the earth and its peoples. So pray to her, praise her, thank her, and be patient. She will prevail.

Twelfth Dance

Now Justice appears to dance with Pallas, for hers is a just war. Rapine and looting may accompany the troops of the enemy, but justice rules over the armies of Queen Christina. And indeed, the Swedish army was one of the first modern armies, regimented and regularly paid to assure that they did not have to live by looting and that they would follow orders. Justice will inspire the rule of law during peacetime. It is the beginning of a new era.

Thirteenth Dance

All the gods convene and disagree about the terms of the peace. At Münster, the delegates negotiating the end of the Thirty Year's War did not agree, either. But Sweden, representing reason, understood both sides. Mars, after all, was born to war. Ordinary people hate it because they suffer so much. Pallas, the goddess of peace, understands both the passions that lead to war and the reasons that speak for peace. The Peace of Westphalia was signed putting Sweden in the ascendancy. And here we find none of the gods taking offense at being ruled by the wise Pallas, fine propaganda for the view that the conquered lands should be happy to be under the rule of Queen Christina's Sweden.

Fourteenth Dance
Mercury comes to proclaim peace, but he is extremely aware of the dangers of fame. Fame, too aware of himself, replies in character by vilifying Mercury as the god of commoners and worse. But in the end they join hands and bow to peace.

Fifteenth Dance
Apollo, the god of political life, enters to dance with Pallas. War is in retreat and Apollo has been called in to reinstate the laws and customs of society. As soon as political order is reestablished, prosperity returns like magic.

Sixteenth Dance
The nine muses enter to enjoin all the ladies, and perhaps all women, to imitate the wise Pallas. All good stems from her wisdom. Queen Christina is a woman, and look what she has accomplished. There is no reason why a woman cannot attain glory in any field of endeavor. If they would turn from trivial pursuits, women could succeed in anything. Descartes, who said he wrote the *Discours* in French so women could read it and who was courtier to two of the most intelligent royal women of his time – Princess Elisabeth and Queen Christina – surely agreed.

Seventeenth Dance
Earth returns renewed, dancing with the three Graces. It is the nature of the earth to rejuvenate itself, and this is the promise that no matter how dark and cold the winter, spring will come.

Descartes, depressed and uncertain in the depths of the Swedish winter, must have clung to this hope. But for him spring never came.

But peace does come to Northern Europe. New woods spring up, and fields are planted. Peasants build new huts, kings new castles, and new life arises everywhere, most poignantly as babies are born to replace the soldiers lost in war.

Eighteenth Dance

It is a two-faced fate in more than one sense. Two-faced Janus looks back horrified on the ravages of war, and forward hopefully to the promise of peace. It is a vision of progress, of continual improvement of the lot of mankind. Like Descartes, Janus can see only chaos and ignorance behind him. But forward, under the wise leadership of Queen Christina, the lower passions will be controlled by the power of will. A new earth and a new order will be established.

Nineteenth Dance

The Cavaliers sing a hymn of praise and prayer to Pallas. She is reason who presides over all human activity, and whose natural tendency is to the good. Whoever follows her must do right. Clearly, the greatest desire of wise subjects should be to be loyal to the queen. Wherever she leads, we should follow, and then whatever we do will be honorable.

But although we have the will to follow our supreme leader, our understanding is limited. Again, the motif is of the queen being the head and her subjects the arms of a mighty body acting for the good. The wisest action is to follow the wisest leader. And now the scene changes again for the third and final act, the Grand Ballet.

Solo Sung before the Grand Ballet

Pallas, all the ladies in the audience, Justice, and the Graces dance in a whirl of marvelous color. Here indeed is the heaven of peace to replace the hell of war. The shining face of peace is revealed as Pallas drops her mask to show Queen Christina dancing. Queen Christina is sovereign of this land in which justice and peace reign.

In a final propagandistic line, a plea is made for ecumenism. We have but one queen and one God. Queen Christina did have hopes for reuniting the Christian churches, and she herself was baptized a Catholic on Christmas Eve, 1654. Descartes was a Catholic, but that he had anything to do with Christina's conversion (as she said he did when asked a leading question long after Descartes had died)[2] is unlikely. But he did say in his Letter to Voetius that Protestants and Catholics worship the same God (AT VIII-2 180), and he certainly believed that the best rule was authoritarian monarchy under the one God.

Chapter 3

DID DESCARTES WRITE
LA NAISSANCE DE LA PAIX?

René Descartes died in Sweden on February 11, 1650, seven weeks before what would have been his fifty-fourth birthday. He was in Stockholm at the behest of Queen Christina, and through the negotiations of Pierre Chanut, the French Resident who became Ambassador to Sweden in December, 1649. Descartes met Chanut in 1644 at the home of his old friend and translator Claude Clerselier (who was Chanut's brother-in-law). Chanut was also probably recommended by the Abbé Claude Picot, who handled Descartes's financial and other affairs in Paris. Chanut and Descartes became close friends rather quickly, and Chanut spent four days with Descartes in Holland in October, 1645, on his way to the Swedish court.

Chanut read the preface of Descartes's *Principia Philosophiae* to Queen Christina, and relayed her questions about philosophy to Descartes. She particularly wanted his opinion on the question of whether an excess of love or of hate caused the most harm. Descartes replied with a classification of the kinds of love, and a description of the usefulness of this passion, concluding that in excess or misunderstanding, love could be more dangerous than hate. Descartes sent Christina a manuscript copy of his *Les Passions de l'Âme*, which he had written in 1646 for Princess Elisabeth of Bohemia. The book was published in November, 1649, with a dedication to Queen Christina, a month after Descartes's arrival in Sweden.

Although Descartes played the role of courtier diligently – his friends joked about his new green velvet suit – and accepted Queen Christina's invitation with great cordiality, he did not in fact want to go to Sweden. He knew that the Queen collected scholars in her court just as she collected scholarly books. He told Chanut he was worried that Queen Christina was not serious about learning philosophy, and then there was the cold. So in April, 1649, when Admiral Flemming arrived in Holland with a ship to take Descartes to Sweden, Descartes put him off, explaining later to Chanut that he had known neither that Flemming was an admiral nor that the Queen had sent him. Flemming returned to Sweden with a boatload of books, but no philosopher. Queen Christina sent him back to Holland again with instructions to get Descartes, and finally the great philosopher boarded ship around the first of September. He actually seemed to enjoy the voyage, fussing with navigation, and he arrived in Stockholm on the first of October, 1649.

From the beginning, Descartes was not happy in Sweden. Queen Christina had very little time for him and gave him six weeks to settle in. Chanut had returned to France for instructions (and promotion to French Ambassador to Sweden), and the Swedish Court was filled with philologists whom Descartes openly scorned. He reported morosely that Sweden was a land of ice and bears, and that in winter there men's thoughts froze like the water. He must have felt that he had been had. His only diversion seems to have been keeping up the daily weather observations that Chanut was recording.

Chanut returned to Stockholm in mid-December, 1649. On January 18, 1650, Chanut caught a cold that soon turned into pneumonia. Descartes was staying at Chanut's house and helped nurse him to health. Then, on February 1, Descartes himself caught a chill. The circumstances are telling. The few times Queen Christina did meet with Descartes, it was at five o'clock in the morning. To be on time, Descartes had to rise at least by four o'clock to get dressed and to cross town in an open carriage. Queen Christina scheduled this early hour even though she knew – or perhaps even because she knew – that Descartes was said to lie in bed until eleven o'clock every morning, meditating.

On February 1, 1650, Descartes took to Queen Christina the text of the charter for a Swedish Academy of Sciences that she had asked him to prepare. In it, Descartes included the provision that foreigners could not be members. He wanted out.

Descartes presented the charter, spent the rest of the day standing in the cold for some ceremonies, and then went home to bed, from which he never arose. His chill turned into pneumonia. At first he refused medication – later there were malicious (but certainly false) rumors that the Queen's doctor poisoned him – and then he took a vicious infusion of hot wine in which tobacco had been dipped that probably hastened his end. On February 11, 1650, at four o'clock in the morning, Descartes died. This is sometimes spoken of as Sweden's only contribution to Modern Philosophy.

Concerning Descartes's time in Sweden, Adrien Baillet tells the following curious story in his *La Vie de Monsieur Des-Cartes* of 1691:

> Meanwhile, M. Descartes was in Stockholm, already tired of the idleness in which he was kept by the Queen, who seemed to have brought him there only for her diversion. The Court was occupied solely with celebrations of the Peace of Münster, and the Queen, who wanted Descartes to play his part, not being able to get him to dance in the ballets, at least succeeded in getting him to compose some French verses for the ball. [Marginal note: They were on the peace, and some fragments of them remain.] He acquitted him-

self of this task in a sprightly manner to please a
Court that already prided itself on its imitation of
French manners. But these verses in no way
demeaned the wisdom of a philosopher of his rank.
They were found too excellent to be the fruits of an
age so advanced, and to have come from an imagina-
tion whose poetic genius he seemed to have smoth-
ered for nearly forty years under the thorn bushes of
algebra and other most dismal sciences. What of
these verses remains for us [Marginal note: As one
can judge from the fragments collected by H. Est.]
serves further to make us judge that M. Descartes,
had he put his philosophy in verse, would have been
more successful than were Thales, Xenophanes,
Empedocles, Epicurus, and Cleanthes among the
Greeks, and Lucretius, Varro, and Boethius among
the Latins. This modest success, although considered
by M. Descartes as a puerility more suited to humili-
ating than to exalting him, perhaps contributed to
increasing further the jealousy of the grammarians
and stupid pedants who fawned upon the Queen, and
who would have derived great profit from the glory
that seemed so trifling and contemptible to M.
Descartes.[1]

Adam and Tannery quote this passage, and continue:

This ballet of Descartes's, of which even Baillet had
only fragments, is unfortunately lost. Morhof also
mentions it in his *Polyhistor*, vol. 2, published in 1692:
". . . Otherwise, [Descartes] was not unpolished in
poetic arts. I have among my papers a choral dance,
Ballet in French, for the birthday of Queen Christina,
La Naissance de la Paix, which Joh. Freinsheimius
translated into the German language." (*Danielis
Georgia* MORHOFII *Polyhistor*, t. II, p. 113, edit. 4a,

Lubecae, sumptibus Petri Beeckmanni, 1747) (AT V 459)[2]

La Naissance de la Paix was published in Stockholm by Jean Janssonius for distribution at the performance of the ballet on Queen Christina's twenty-third birthday, December 8, 1649, although it was actually performed on December 9, 1649. Queen Christina herself is said to have danced the role of Pallas Athena. A German translation by Johannnes Freinsheimius and a Swedish version by Georg Stiernhielm were also prepared for the audience to follow during the performance.

In 1691, Baillet knew only of fragments of the ballet, and he does not give its name. The text was not published by Adam and Tannery in their *Oeuvres de Descartes* (1897–1913). Then in 1920, a slightly inaccurate version of the ballet was published in *La Revue de Genève*, with a commentary by Albert Thibaudet and a comment by Johan Nordström, who examined two copies of the printed text in the Carolina Rediviva in Uppsala.[3] A more accurate version has been printed in the *Samlade Skrifter av Georg Stiernhielm*.[4] There is also a copy of the 1649 original in the Kungliga Biblioteket in Stockholm and a pristine copy – as though published yesterday – in the Herzog August Bibliothek in Wolfenbüttel.

The *Revue de Genève* text of *La Naissance de la Paix* is reprinted in the Nouvelle Présentation of Adam and Tannery edited by Pierre Costabel. It is included in a section titled "Documents d'origines diverses II" with only the following brief note: "This ballet was composed by Descartes on the occasion of the birthday of Queen Christina and of the celebrations of the peace [of Westphalia] that occasioned the ballet. We know from both Descartes and contemporary accounts that the ballet's performance was postponed until the following day, 9/19 December 1649) (cf. *supra*, p. 457, I, 16). Descartes's text was thought to be lost, and Baillet himself knew only a few fragments of it" (cf. *supra*, p. 459). (AT V 616–627)

Costabel gives no indication that *La Naissance de la Paix* was published as a booklet in Stockholm by Jean Janssonius in 1649, nor does he say that, if Descartes wrote it, it is the last of Descartes's works published during his lifetime. In fact, because the texts of ballets were printed for ballet audiences to read during performances, the published booklet must have been available to Descartes on December 8, 1649.

There does not appear to be a copy of the original in the Bibliothèque Nationale in Paris, but the text is available there in a book by Louis Aragon titled *La Naissance de la Paix*, which consists of the ballet verses interspersed with prose by Aragon.[5] Aragon's prose sets the scenes with many stage directions. Aragon's version was presented on French radio in 1946.[6] This suggests that there may be an original copy of the ballet somewhere in Paris.

La Naissance de la Paix is an allegorical celebration of the Peace of Westphalia, which was signed in Münster on October 24, 1648. Sweden emerged from these negotiations more or less as victor of the Thirty Years' War, collecting many spoils of war and annexing a large amount of territory, including Pomerania. Baillet says that a promise of a pension and a castle in Pomerania is one of the devices Queen Christina used to lure Descartes into her Court.

Sweden may have been a land of ice and bears, but it was far from being culturally backward. According to Beijer,[7] Queen Christina had sent Count Magnus Gabriel de la Gardie to France in 1646 to investigate the latest equipment and techniques of the theater. De la Gardie concluded a contract with Antonio Brunati, who had learned theater technique and architecture in Italy. Brunati started building a theater at the castle in Stockholm in 1647, with a *salle de ballet* of thirty-four by eighty meters. Again, according to Beijer, the result was as grand and as technically advanced as anything in Europe. The inauguration was in April, 1649, with *Les Passions Victorieuses et Vaincues*, a very Cartesian and Corneillean theme, followed in

October by *Le Vaincu de Diane*, which ballets allegorically justify Queen Christina's decision to be her own woman and not to marry.[8]

According to Stewart, a ballet of the time was either *Grand* with thirty *entrées*, *Beau* with thirteen to twenty *entrées*, or *Petit* with ten or twelve *entrées*.[9] *La Naissance de la Paix* is thus a *Beau Ballet*, having twenty *entrées*, not including the solo sung at the beginning but including the *grand ballet* (not to be confused with *Grand*) at the end, in which all the women danced (following continental practice in which the *grand ballet* was danced only by men or only by women).

La Naissance de la Paix is separated into the traditional three acts, with a solo to be sung before each. There was a change of scene for each act. The texts of the songs and of the verses were not recited, but were provided to the audience in a printed program. The verses describe the scenes acted in pantomime by professional dancers. As was usual, realistic and grotesque *entrées* alternate. For the performance, the French text was distributed along with the German translation by Johannes Freinsheimius, *Des Friedens Geburts-tag*, and the Swedish version by Georg Stiernhielm, *Freds-Afl*.

The music for the solos was probably written by Andreas Duben, who became Master of the Queen's Music in 1640, but according to Stewart,[10] the instrumental music for the dances was probably composed by the musicians, as being beneath the dignity of distinguished composers. The dances were choreographed by the French ballet master Antoine de Beaulieu, who had been in the court since 1638. Beijer says that it is probable that *Panique Terreur* was danced by the ballet master himself.[11] The ballet costumes were very rich, and this act would have been danced in a ferocious-looking mask.

Did Descartes actually write *La Naissance de la Paix*? No. There is no evidence whatsoever that Descartes wrote *La Naissance de la Paix*. The attribution of authorship to him is based on a single sentence (no one has ever cited any other evidence) that Descartes added as a postscript to his letter of December 8, 1649, to M. de Flessel, Vicomte de Brégy, Conseiller du Roy en ses Conseils, Ambassadeur de France en Pologne. The Vicomte de Brégy was in Stockholm on a mission when Descartes arrived in October. They met and became friends. De Brégy then returned to Paris because his father had died. Descartes wrote him with a bit of news, and here is the one-sentence postscript on which the myth of Descartes's authorship of *La Naissance de la Paix* is based:

"Afin que la grosseur de ce pacquet empesche qu'il ne soit aysé a égarer, j'y adiouste les vers d'un balet qui sera dansé icy demain au soir."

"So that the size of this parcel will keep it from easily going astray, I have added the verses of a ballet that will be danced here tomorrow evening." (AT V 457)

There is no question but that the verses referred to are the printed version of *La Naissance de la Paix*, which was to be performed "tomorrow evening," December 9, 1649. Descartes's offhand way with them might be interpreted as a modest way of including something he had written, but there is no reason here to suppose that Descartes meant more than he said. There is a perfectly adequate explanation for why Descartes sent de Brégy a copy of *La Naissance de la Paix*. De Brégy was very interested in the political content of the court ballets. He went to some length to see them. This is documented in a letter from Johan Ekebald, who wrote to his father from Stockholm on October 23, 1649:

> Her Majesty did not attend the funeral (of the wife of the Chancellor) because of an indisposition and also because she wanted to hasten the preparation for the ballet [*La Diane Victorieuse*], because of this French ambassador [identified as de Brégy], who is in a

hurry to leave Sweden before the water freezes but is delaying his departure to see the ballet first.[12]

It is probable that Descartes attended *La Diane Victorieuse* with de Brégy and that he sent him the text of *La Naissance de la Paix* because he knew that de Brégy would like to have it. De Brégy might have even asked that it be sent, in which case Descartes's postscript might express his amusement at de Brégy's interest. But because it is certain that de Brégy had serious interest in the political content of the ballet, Descartes's dismissive reference to the ballet could have been a matter of discretion.

Is this enough to attribute authorship of the ballet to Descartes? One suggestion that it is not derives from the following. Descartes had with him in Sweden papers and journals that went back as far as 1619. He kept so many papers that if he had written *La Naissance de la Paix*, one would expect to find a copy of manuscript or at least some notes pertaining to the ballet in his papers. But nothing pertaining to *La Naissance de la Paix* is listed in the inventory made of Descartes's papers in Sweden after his death (AT V 1–14).

Nor, incidentally, is there any listing in that inventory of the chapters of the comedy that Baillet says Descartes wrote for amusement in Sweden:

> We find also among M. Descartes's manuscripts . . . a sort of French comedy, which he wrote in prose mixed with some verse during his stay in the Swedish Court. This was one of the fruits of the idleness in which the Queen kept him during the absence of the French Ambassador, whose return she was awaiting. The play is incomplete, and the fourth act appears not to be finished. It has the air of a Pastoral or a woodland Fable. But although he seems to have wanted to express the love of Wisdom, the search for Truth,

and the study of Philosophy with the allegorical discourse of his characters, one can say that all this mys-
tification will carry little weight with the Public as
long as it can enjoy M. Descartes's other writings in
which he has explained himself without mysteries.
   It is . . . a French comedy that is somewhat mysti-
fying, but respectable, and in the style of the Ancients
[Marginal note: We have this comedy in manuscript.],
which he wrote two months before his death in
Sweden, in addition to the verse and prose of the ballet on the peace of Münster, of which we have spoken
elsewhere. (AT V 484)

Leibniz wrote a summary of this comedy based on his reading
of a copy given to him by Clerselier in 1676 (AT VXI 661–662).
It is set in Iceland, and one character is "the Tyrant of
Stockholm." But even if the manuscript of this lost comedy was
in Descartes's handwriting, as Baillet implies, this would not
constitute evidence that Descartes may also have written the
ballet. However, the comedy is discussed by Baillet along with a
discussion of "a small treatise describing how to fence under
the title of *L'Art d'Escrime*[13] that Descartes wrote in his youth.
This suggests that the comedy could also be a piece of juvenil-
ia. Baillet may have dated its composition in October and
November, 1649, because it is set in Iceland and one of the characters is the Tyrant of Stockholm.
   Did Descartes actually spend his first two months in Sweden
composing a twenty-act ballet and nearly four acts of a comedy?
It seems that he did compose the comedy at some time or other.
But would Descartes have started writing poetry at the age of
fifty-three in Sweden? If he did, then he had forgotten what he
wrote on February 17, 1645, to Constantin Huygens:

   Monsieur,
      The Poem that you have done me the favor of send-
   ing to me is so excellent, and contains a syllogism so

ingeniously formed in the style of the School, that seeing you philosophize so well in verse, I almost found myself in a humor to want also to philosophize in verse in an attempt to respond to your courtesies. But remembering that Socrates wrote verse only when he was approaching death, for fear that this would likewise be a bad augury for me, and that one might say in Flemish that I was veygh [at the point of death], I have refrained." (AT IV 776–777)

I do not think Descartes wrote poetry in Sweden, but if he did, his premonitions of four years earlier might seem to have substance.

There are several further lines of argument against Descartes's writing *La Naissance de la Paix*. First, it is the third in a series of five ballets with texts in verse performed in 1649 and 1650 in the Stockholm court on political themes very dear to Queen Christina's heart and mind. One was performed before Descartes arrived there, two while he was in the Court, and two after his death. They are:

1. *Les Passions Victorieuses et Vaincues*, April, 1649, on the subjection of the erotic passions in order for the Queen to rule more fairly and effectively.
2. *Le Vaincu de Diane/La Diane Victorieuse*, by Hélie Poirier, performed twice in November, 1649, on the decision of the queen not to marry.
3. *La Naissance de la Paix*, December, 1649, on the triumph of Pallas, the goddess of peace, over Mars, the god of war, and the imposition of peaceful rule by the Queen.
4. *La Pompe de la Felicité*, by Charles de Beys, October, 1650, on the domination of both Mars, the god of war, and Cupid, the god of love, by Felicité, who maintains peace.
5. *Parnasse Triomphant*, January, 1651, on the benefits of peace.

In terms of style, rhyme schemes, characterization, and themat-
ic development, one could argue that Hélie Poirier wrote *Les
Passions Victorieuses et Vaincues,* and that Charles de Beys
wrote *Parnasse Triomphant,* and that either Poirier or de Beys
wrote *La Naissance de la Paix.* I argue that the author of *La
Naissance de la Paix* was Poirier. There is evidence that Poirier
was in the Court at the time *La Naissance de la Paix* was composed and performed, and Stewart says that "according to an
old note in the library at Uppsala authorship of the ballet was
ascribed to Poirier."[14] I have seen the note, which is in the manuscript *Palmsköldiana* 361:675 in the Carolina Rediviva, the
Uppsala Universitetsbibliotek.[15] In it *La Naissance de la Paix* is
listed with *Le Vaincu de Diane* as a work by Poirier. The
Palmsköldiana collection was acquired by the library in 1724.
There is an Amsterdam watermark in the paper on which the
Poirier entry is written. *La Naissance de la Paix* is also attrib-
uted to Poirier by Carl Silfverstolpe in 1889[16] and by Johan
Grönstedt in 1911.[17] Silfverstolpe's attribution of authorship to
Poirier is strong circumstantial evidence given that
Silfverstolpe's article is on Antoine de Beaulieu, the ballet mas-
ter for *La Naissance de la Paix.* Perhaps Silfverstolpe had docu-
mentary proof that may still turn up.

We know that Poirier wrote *Le Vaincu de Diane* because it
was published in 1649 by Jean Janssonius in Stockholm with
Hélie Poirier's name printed as author on the cover. Both *Les
Passions Victorieuses et Vaincues* and *La Naissance de la Paix*
were published in 1649 by Jean Janssonius, but with no author
indicated. Of course, Descartes had a well-known penchant for
anonymity in the publishing of his works. But we cannot argue
that if Poirier were the author, one would expect his name to be
printed as author, because his name is missing not only from
Les Passions Victorieuses et Vaincues, which he probably wrote,
but also from a separate 1649 printing of his *Le Vaincu de Diane*
titled *La Diane Victoreuse* that differs only slightly from *Le
Vaincu de Diane* (for example, the last six lines are missing),

which we know he wrote. In fact, as I remark above, stylistic evidence indicates that Poirier wrote all three of these ballets.

But again, Charles de Beys has a similar style. And it is striking that Thibaudet, assuming that Descartes wrote *La Naissance de la Paix*, remarks that "Descartes is certainly nearer to the poetry of Scarron, Théophile, and Saint-Amand than to that of Corneille,"[18] and that Gustafsson notes that Charles de Beys is a "relatively little known French poet who belongs to the circle of Scarron and Saint-Amand who wrote plays, burlesques, and drinking songs."[19] Such a poet could certainly have written the following verse for the dance of the crippled soldiers in *La Naissance de la Paix*:

Qui voit comme nous sommes faits
Who sees how we have been undone

Et pense que la guerre est belle,
Yet praises war in beauty's name,

Ou qu'elle vaut mieux que la Paix,
Thinks Peace in worth the lesser one,

Est estropié de ceruelle.
Is crippled badly in his brain."[20]

Also, the themes of *La Naissance de la Paix* and of *La Pompe de Felicité* are almost the same. I do tend toward de Beys on these grounds, but there is no documentary evidence that he wrote *La Naissance de la Paix*, while there is the note in the Uppsala University Library that Poirier did.

Stewart seems uneasy about Descartes's authorship, but says "there can be no reasonable doubt, since we have the testimony of [Johannes] Freinsheimius [Queen Christina's librarian and translator of the German version of the ballet] and Morhof and the independent testimony of Baillet."[21] The trouble

is that Stewart cites for Freinsheimus's "testimony" only
Morhof's *Polyhistor* published in 1692, in which Morhof says
that Freinsheimius translated the ballet into German from
Descartes's French. And Morhof's source could have been
Baillet's *La Vie de Monsieur Des-Cartes*, published in 1691, in
which the "evidence" is only that Descartes sent a copy of it to
the Vicomte de Brégy on December 8, 1649, to give bulk to a
package so it would not get lost. Neither Morhof nor Baillet
cites any actual evidence that Descartes wrote the ballet. It is
possible that Baillet had not even seen fragments of the ballet,
for he speaks of the ballet as consisting of both "verse and
prose,"[22] which is true of the comedy, but not of the ballet. And
of the comedy, he says "We have this comedy in manuscript."[23]
This suggests that Baillet saw the comedy but not the ballet.

Sven Delblanc[24] has challenged Rolf Lindborg's[25] assumption
that Descartes wrote *La Naissance de la Paix*. Delblanc argues
that the Swedish version of the ballet by the father of Swedish
poetry, Georg Stiernhielm, whose has always been said to be a
translation of, or, rather, inspired by, the French text, is actually
the original, and that the French version is the translation.
Beijer says that Stiernhielm's "Swedish verses . . . are justly celebrated in the literary history of the country and have often
been reprinted."[26] Neither is true of the French version, which,
despite Baillet's claim, is not good poetry. Delblanc apparently
thinks that the version that is the best poetry has to be the original, a shaky principle of attribution. I agree with Delblanc that
Descartes did not write the original version of the ballet, but neither did Stiernhielm.

But suppose Stiernhielm did write the first version and
Descartes translated it. It seems unlikely that Descartes knew
Swedish that well (or at all), but Freinsheimius, who was
Descartes's friend, could have helped him get the sense. The
French and Swedish versions are so different that if one did
come from the other, it had to be an adaptation, not a transla-
tion. The main evidence that the French version is the original

is that Freinsheimius's German version closely follows the French text. If Stiernhielm's Swedish version had been the original, surely Freinsheimius would have followed it rather than the French version to make his nearly literal German translation. And also, of course, it *was* a French ballet. The verses of the other four ballets in the series are in French (with some verses in Spanish in *Les Passions Victorievses et Vaincves*). Whether or not Descartes wrote *La Naissance de la Paix*, the French version is surely the original.

Besides the *Palmsköldiana* attribution of *La Naissance de la Paix* to Poirier, the strongest argument against Descartes's authorship is based on content. Lars Gustafsson warns against taking the content of any of the court ballets as expressing the ideas of their authors. These ballets often have strong political messages, and this is certainly true of Poirier's *Les Passions Victorievses et Vaincves* and *Le Vaincu de Diane*, which glorify the Virgin Queen. As Gustafsson says, "The ballets of the last period plead without ambiguity the cause of the personal politics of the Queen."[27] This includes *La Naissance de la Paix*. The ideas in these ballets convey Queen Christina's political convictions and machinations. She saw and used brilliantly the great potential of the ballets as propaganda. In general, they promote the view that Queen Christina and Sweden are the guardians of peace in Europe, and specifically they provide justification for Christina's determination not to marry and even prefigure her abdication. Whoever wrote them had either to be in the employ of or close to the Queen, and Descartes was neither. It is more likely that the Queen would assign the writing of a political allegory to a professional versifier than to a new courtier.

Poirier was a professional who could catch Queen Christina's intent quickly and turn it into verse. What Baillet and others such as Geneviève Rodis-Lewis[28] forget is that the verses of ballets such as these cannot just be tossed off by some amateur, but are the honed work of professionals. Descartes was a great philosopher, but it is absurd to suggest (as Baillet does) that he just sat down and churned out these verses to the envy of other members of the court.

Gilbert Louise says that as a gentleman, as an amateur of poetry and of music, as a man who would have liked to be counselor to the Queen, as a quasi-diplomat from France to Sweden, and, finally, as a physiological philosopher of the passions, Descartes was capable of writing the ballet and would have been well disposed toward doing so. Well, just possibly.

But when Louise continues that "When one brings these [political] considerations to the verses of the ballet, one can only suppose the complicity of Christina and Descartes; this is what we think,"[29] I respond that exactly the hypothesis of this complicity provides an argument against Descartes's authorship, because there is no evidence that the Queen confided her political ambitions to Descartes. On the other hand, a professional such as Poirier could express the ideas without any need to assume complicity. He was just doing his job.

John M. Morris, like Louise, thinks that "the ballet was a musical dramatization of the philosophical work [*Passions de l'âme*], in which each of the major passions becomes a character on the stage."[30] This may well *seem* to be the case. The point is that if one follows Louise's admonition that "to interpret the text of the ballet, we will rely upon the hypothesis of an understanding between Descartes and Christina," then the ballet certainly appears to be "in accord with the political thoughts of Descartes."[31] But it is also in accord with the commonplace maxims of Stoicism, which was Christina's favored philosophy.

And that their interpretation is based on the *assumption* that Descartes wrote the ballet is precisely how my method differs from that of Louise and Morris. I look for external evidence that Descartes is the author of the ballet, and I find none. Louise and Morris *suppose* that Descartes is the author, and on this hypothesis they look in the ballet for internal evidence, and they find it. But this internal "evidence" is not a proof independent of their supposition. You can find almost anything in a text if you look for it on the assumption that it is there.

If Descartes is the author, then it seems reasonable to think that the text of the ballet would reflect Descartes's position. But the prior question is to know whether or not Descartes is the author. The sole external "evidence" cited by Louise (Morris cites no external evidence) is that Descartes sent a copy of the ballet to de Brégy, and I have already shown that this is not sufficient.

I conclude that the supposition that Descartes is the author of the ballet should be rejected precisely because this supposition leads to the inference "that Descartes had cleverly adjusted it to the political situation of the Swedish court at that moment in a manner favorable to the Queen."[32] We know that Descartes was not in the employ of the Queen as a professional versifier, and there is no evidence that Descartes enjoyed the confidence of the Queen required to support the supposition that the internal content of the ballet constitutes evidence that Descartes is its author.

The political content and use of the five ballets in series, however, is just what constitutes my main positive reason for doubting that Descartes wrote *La Naissance de la Paix*. (The main negative reason, of course, is that there is no evidence that he did.) I believe that it is important to determine whether or not Descartes wrote it, for if he did, then it shows him involved in Queen Christina's political affairs, and could be used to infer something about Descartes's own political philosophy. But Descartes arrived in Stockholm early in October, only two months before the ballet was performed. He had by then barely met the Queen. As remarked above, on his arrival she gave him six weeks to settle in, and then she went away from Stockholm. Would she have delegated the writing of this important political statement – a celebration of Sweden's role in the Peace of Westphalia and of her intentions to maintain peace – to

an untried foreigner, a Catholic, and a new courtier known neither for composing ballets nor for writing verse? Virtually at
their first meeting? It seems highly unlikely. And even if in her
perverse way she had told Descartes to write it – I repeat that
there is no evidence that she did – would he have had time?
Wouldn't Freinsheimius (who soon became Descartes's friend)
have just arranged quietly to have Poirier (or de Beys) – a prac-
ticed author of political ballet verse – write it for him? I think *La
Naissance de la Paix* must have been written by Hélie Poirier,
who definitely wrote *Le vaincu de Diane* and probably wrote *Les
Passions Victorieuses et Vaincues* in this series of five ballets that,
as I remark above, are virtual doctrinal statements of Queen
Christina's theories about Swedish politics and her role as
Queen. Poirier demonstrably could have written *La Naissance
de la Paix*. Descartes? I don't say categorically that he couldn't
have: I say he didn't. Too bad for those of us who would like to
use it to construct a political philosophy for Descartes.

In *La Naissance de la Paix*, the goddess of peace, Pallas, triumphs over the god of war, Mars. As Gustafsson analyses the
ballet, it is propaganda to the effect that for Queen Christina,
war should not be for conquest, but for justice. Queen Christina
triumphs over love and hate: "Christina is celebrated in the alle-
gories of the court's festivities as the august promoter of universal ethical order."[33] The force of will guided by reason establish-
es universal peace and order. This stress on will guided by reason is Cartesian, but on the other hand, the Stoics – who also
stressed will and reason – were Queen Christina's favorite
philosophers. Will and reason subordinating desire and the passions is also a central theme of Corneille's plays, which all the
court knew.

Why did Baillet attribute authorship of *La Naissance de la
Paix* to Descartes on so little evidence? I suspect it is for the
same reason that he and others said that Descartes participated
in the Battle of White Mountain, marched on La Rochelle, and
wrote "Sonnet sur la Mort du Roy Henry le Grand, et sur la

descouverte de quelques nouvelles Planettes ou estoiles errantes autour de Jupiter, faite l'Année d'icelle par Galilée célébre Mathematicien du grand duc de Florence" at La Flèche when he was fourteen years old: he happened to be in Poland, and France, and La Flèche at the appropriate times. But in fact there is no more evidence that Descartes wrote *La Naissance de la Paix* than there is that he lived the life of Dimitri Davidenko's super-hero cavalier, *Descartes le scandaleux.*[34]

It was a bizarre end for a great philosopher. Descartes's fondest hope was that he might find – in his medical research – a method for prolonging human life. He said he liked Italy but would not settle there because it was too hot and the air was unhealthy. He left the turmoil and distractions of Paris to spend most of his adult life in tranquil Holland. His days in The Netherlands were ordered, calm, and constant. But he was look-ing for something more. In 1647, he had been awarded a Royal pension of 3,000 livres a year, but when he went to Paris in 1648, he found that no money was forthcoming (AT XII 458ff). He complained that people merely wanted to gawk at him, as though he were some exotic animal, like an elephant or a pan-ther (AT XII 467). And this, I am afraid, is just how Queen Christina saw him.[35] She, too, offered a pension, and bought him. There is no evidence that he was ever paid.

And so, one might say, Descartes was undone by the whim of an inconstant queen. On the one hand, Christina was one of the most powerful, clever, and effective monarchs in Europe. On the other hand, she seemed never able to settle on anything. She did make some spectacular decisions – to abdicate, to con-vert to Catholicism, and to live in Rome. But she never carried through any great project on her own. In the short run, she was a superb character for one of Corneille's plays, for she did decide that her cousin Karl Gustav would be a more appropriate ruler for Sweden than herself, and she forced her crown on him. In the long run, she dallied with this and that, turning out to be serious about neither philosophy nor religion. The wise Pallas of *La Naissance de la Paix* caused disruption wherever she went. Her dilettantism ended Descartes's life.

But "Who, then, is this Hélie Poirier, Parisian?" asks Frédéric Lachèvre in his *Glanes bibliographiques et littéraires*,[36] and he replies: "The *Dictionaires biographiques* say nothing about him, and only *France Protestant* devotes a few lines to him. It cites him as being a protestant, translator of a Latin work by Godefroy Hotton, a refugee in The Netherlands because of religion. However, Poirier did not expatriate himself because he was born a Calvinist, as a Calvinist by birth would not have been "Prior of Argenteuil."[37]

Poirier published *Les Amours de Mélisse, Poésie Amoureuse et Religieuse* in 1625, and *La Journée du Pénitent Composée de Méditations Psalmes, et Litanies en Vers François* in 1627. In 1634, he was Curé of Chenevières-sur-Marne. According to Lachèvre, in 1640, when Poirier was forty years old,

> One Melissa, fully aware of her charms and expert in the matter, made the poor curé fall into error, and the scandal in a small village such as Chenevières-sur-Marne made it necessary for him to throw his cassock to the winds and leave France. He chose The Netherlands in preference to the Genevan Republic, which was reputed to be not very hospitable.[38]

In Amsterdam in 1641, Poirier translated Erasmus's *Encomium Moriae* and *Tactiques d'AElian* at the request of Frédéric Henri, Prince of Orange, who was also the protector of Descartes, and who died on March 14, 1647, to some extent leaving Descartes in the lurch, and perhaps Poirier, too.

In 1646, Poirier wrote some verses for the chancellor of Sweden, Oxenstern, and also in 1646, he dedicated *Les Soupirs Salutaires* to Queen Christina. In 1647, Poirier translated a book of Godefroy Hötton, *De l'Union et Réconciliation des Äglises Évangéliques de l'Europe: ou des Moyens d'Ätablir Entre Elles une Tolérance et Charité*, in which Hötton treats an ecumenical theme dear to the heart of Queen Christina. In 1648, Poirier translated the Dutch military engineer Mathias Dögen's *L'Architecture Militaire Moderne, ou Fortification*, which he dedicated to William, Prince of Orange, a subject Descartes had been interested in when he was young. In 1648, Poirier also published *Deux Harangues Panégyriques*, one on peace and the other on concord, with a translation of Grotius's treatise *De l'Antiquité de la République des Hollandais*.

In a note on Hélie Poirier, H. W. Van Tricht makes some comments on the idiosyncratic orthography of Poirier, which tended to be phonetic, and he identifies Poirier as the French translator of Erasmus's *La Louange de la Sottise* (*Encomium Moriae*) on orthographic evidence.[39] *La Naissance de la Paix* is in normal orthography, but one cannot infer from this that Poirier was not its author, since *Le Vaincu de Diane/La Diane Victorievse*, which Poirier wrote, is also in normal orthography. Van Tricht gives no indication that Poirier was in Sweden, other than mentioning the two versions of the *Diane* ballet published in Stockholm in 1649.

Lachèvre makes no reference to the residence in Sweden of Hélie Poirier, Parisian, nor to the ballet *Vaincu de Diane/La Diane Victorievse*. The ballet should be a major piece of evidence that he was in Stockholm in 1649. But according to copies of two letters from Poirier in the collection of Johan Nordström in the Carolina Rediviva in Uppsala, Poirier was in Amsterdam on May 30, 1648, and January 17, 1649,[40] and there is no indication in these letters that Poirier had any intention of going to Sweden.

Poirier did go to Sweden, however, for in a letter of December 9, 1649, to Thuillierie (French Ambassador to the United Provinces), de Brasset (the French Resident) remarks that Poirier drowned in a shipwreck on his return from Stockholm. Then de Brasset goes on to say that Poirier was a man "that I would have expected to drown in wine rather than in the Baltic Sea."[41]

Thus Poirier was in Sweden at the right time. If he wrote the ballet, he was paid for it, so I looked in the Royal Household Records, and on December 9, 1649, a lump sum was paid to the ballet master, Antoine de Beaulieu. The name of the author of the ballet is not given. I have found no absolute proof that Poirier wrote *La Naissance de la Paix*, but the circumstantial evidence that he did is far greater than the one piece of circumstantial evidence – the copy mailed to de Brégy – that its author was Descartes.

Chapter 4

DESCARTES'S DOCTRINE OF THE WILL

"It is only the will, or freedom of choice, which I experience within me to be so great that the idea of any greater faculty is beyond my grasp; so much so that it is above all in virtue of the will that I understand myself to bear in some way the image and likeness of God." (CSM II 40; AT VIII 57)

– René Descartes, *Meditations*

A. The Power of the Will

In the Fourth Meditation, Descartes says that error arises because we abuse our infinite power of willing to affirm or deny beyond the limits justified by our finite knowledge. To avoid this, we should make judgments only when we have sufficient knowledge about the matters at hand. Of course in life we often must act on insufficient knowledge, and in these cases we should chose what is most probable. If we must act when there is no ground whatsoever for choice, at least we should take a consistent course.

If our understanding is limited, so also are the abilities of our bodies. My will power, in "the image and likeness of God" is infinite, but my power to move my body is limited. I can will to rise off the floor and float across the room, to run the mile in three minutes, or to lift a ton, but none of these things happen when I will them. It is not a matter of my not straining hard enough, for I strain as hard as I can. And if the power of my willing is infinite, then my act of willing should be equally easy in any case, whether it is in the matter of simply willing to raise my arm or willing to fly like Superman.

There do, however, seem to be occasions on which one strains one's will. Anyone who has been a gymnast or a high jumper or who has done a very difficult thing recognizes that you must work yourself up to some physical actions, and that there is a state of willful determination that exceeds that of ordinary acts of willing. In such cases, strength of will often is determinative of whether or not you accomplish something that you can just barely do at the limits of your physical ability. Difficult intellectual work also requires a stiff tightening up of will power, to resist distractions, to keep your mind on the subject, to think as hard as you can about the problem or subject in question. You can force your body and your mind to perform at their limits, but doing so requires an extremely intense concentration of will power. Descartes's instructions for how to prepare for reading his *Meditations* – set aside free time, relax, put aside other problems – are calculated to help you get into a state of mind so you can concentrate on the problems he presents there. But refining and deploying the will most efficently is much more complicated than that.

Descartes begins by discussing bodily motions that give rise to mental passions that lead in turn to mental desires concerning the body (henceforth: bodily desires). In *Les Passions de l'Âme*, Descartes says that "simply by willing something it [the soul] brings it about that the little [pineal] gland to which it is closely joined moves in the manner required to produce the [bodily] effect corresponding to this volition" (CSM I 343; AT XI

360). Of course if the body is physically incapable of doing what is willed, e.g., flying, then nothing happens. More important than the ability to will positive bodily movements, however, is the negative ability to curb bodily movements that result from the passions. Descartes says that "the strongest souls belong to those in whom the will by nature can most easily conquer the passions and stop the bodily movements that accompany them" (CSM I 347; AT XI 367–368). Unfortunately, "it is easy to believe that the souls that God puts into our bodies are not equally noble and strong" (CSM I 394; AT XI 453). There are "advantages we possess from birth – those of the soul or . . . the body" (CSM I 394; AT XI 467) that differ from person to person. In particular, members of the nobility have superior souls and bodies. (CSM I 388; AT XI 453)

Just how much control the soul has over the will is very important to Descartes. He says that "I see only one thing in us that could give us good reason for esteeming ourselves, namely, the exercise of our free will and the control we have over our volitions" (CSM I 384; AT XI 445). But when Descartes says that free will "renders us in a certain way like God by making us masters of ourselves, provided we do not lose the rights it gives us through timidity" (CSM I 384; AT XI 445), he indicates that our control of the will has limits. In other words, the will is infinitely strong, but the soul is finitely weak. The soul has some command of the will, but this control is limited, and it is to the question of how and just how much the soul can control the will that I now turn.

Obviously, if free will were all powerful in the sense of being impervious to restraint, so that all we had to do was switch it on or off, then there would be no question either of having to work it up or of its being diverted by the passions. But because it is not always easy to exert one's will, its infinite nature must be in its scope of application, and in its being total when applied, rather than in our ability to deploy it, or in its power to bring about anything we will. Theoretically, we can will anything, that is, the scope or field over which we can will is infinite. But although we can will anything, what we can do is limited by the powers of our body and soul or mind. Both mind and body are limited as finite substances, and beyond this they can be further defective. For example, I may be of a fearful nature so that there are things I actually could do that I do not do because I cannot bring myself to will to do them. More than that, not only do I sometimes will wrongly because of lack of knowledge, if I have a weak mind I may reason poorly, or if I have a bad nature I may will perverse actions, and if I am in a lustful state, I may give in to desires that cause me to will sinful things.

B. Control of the Body

Descartes says we can improve our bodies through healthful living, and thus increase our ability to do certain things. We can improve our reason by practice and our minds by ruling the mental passions that "govern our behavior by producing [bodily] desire in us [in our minds]" (CSM I 379; AT XI 436). That is, bodily desires that derive from passions control our behavior, so we must control our passions. Descartes gives elaborate and crucial instructions concerning how to overcome bodily desires by controlling our passions.

According to Descartes, the main passions that cause bodily desires are joy, love, sadness, and hatred: "these [mental] passions cannot lead us to perform any action except by means of the [bodily] desire they produce, and it is this [bodily] desire that we should take particular care to control" (CSM I 379; AT XI 436).

We must control our bodily desires because they trigger volitions that lead to bodily motions. Volitions are "actions of the soul" (CSM I 335; AT XI 343). That is:

> Of the two kinds of thought I have distinguished in the soul – the first is actions, i.e., its volitions, and the second its passions, taking this word in its most gen-

eral sense to include every kind of perception – the former [volitions] are absolutely within its [the soul's] power and can be changed only indirectly by the body, whereas the latter [passions] are absolutely dependent on the actions [bodily motions] that produce them, and can be changed by the soul only indirectly, except when it is itself their cause. And the activity of the soul consists entirely in the fact that simply by willing something it brings it about that the little [pineal] gland to which it is closely joined moves in the manner required to produce the effect corresponding to this volition. (CSM I 343; AT XI 359–360)

Thus some volitions are completely under the control of the mind, but others are controlled by passions that are caused by bodily motions, which passions give rise to bodily desires. That is, "the principal effect of all the human passions is that they move and dispose the soul to want the things for which they prepare the body [i.e., have bodily desires]. Thus the feeling [passion] of fear moves the soul to want to flee, that of courage to want to fight, and similarly with the others" (CSM I 343; AT XI 359). Unless diverted by reasoning, the soul wills to satisfy the bodily desires caused by its passions, which in turn were caused by bodily motions. But volitions can also be caused directly by the soul. It is crucial for Descartes that if the mind is to have any control of the will, it must be able to override the influence of bodily desires.

Bodily desires arise from passions. Passions are generated by the body's interaction with material objects in the world. In detail, passions are caused by external bodies impacting on the sense organs to cause animal (material) spirits to flow through the nerves to enter the pores in the brain where they "produce in the [pineal] gland a particular movement which is ordained by nature to make the soul feel this [or that] passion" (CSM I 341; AT XI 357). Then the passions cause bodily desires, which

– when not restrained – trigger volitions to bodily action calculated to satisfy those desires.

To control bodily desires, the soul must replace the bodily motions that cause, e.g., the passion of fear, by the bodily motions that cause, e.g., the passion of courage. Because the passions are caused by the movements of one's body acting on the pineal gland, the passions can be altered by changing the movements of one's body. The mind can change bodily movements by causing certain motions in the pineal gland that in turn cause certain motions in one's body. That is, the pineal gland is the common center of reception of information about the movements of one's body and of control of bodily motions in response to this information. Stimulus terminates in the pineal gland and response originates there on the basis of this stimulus. The stimulus affecting the pineal gland can come either from one's body or one's mind, and when it comes from one's mind it overrides the stimulus from one's body. Bodily stimulus comes from mechanical interaction of one's body with material things, and the bodily response to it is automatic, but "the activity of the soul consists entirely in the fact that simply by willing something it brings about that the little [pineal] gland to which it is closely joined moves in the manner required to produce the effect corresponding to this volition" (CSM I 343; AT XI 360).

Thus, if my body is trembling through the shock of seeing the enemy suddenly approaching, this trembling affects my pineal gland in such a way as to give rise in my mind to the passion of fear, which in turn causes me to desire to flee. And if nothing interferes, I (my mind) will respond to this bodily desire by willing to satisfy it, that is, to flee. However, my reason may make me have the conflicting desire to fight, and so I can will to have courage by causing my pineal gland to move in such a way as to stop my body's trembling and to ready my muscles for battle. This bodily state, then, in turn affects the pineal gland anew to cause it now to give rise to the passion of courage in my mind, which in turn causes me to desire to fight. Thus my mental desire to advance causes a bodily state that in turn causes me to have a mental desire to advance, and then I do will to advance rather than to retreat.

Now why could I not just will myself to fight straight off? The reason is that as long as my bodily state (trembling and so on) sends a message to the pineal gland that gives rise in my mind to the passion of fear and the resultant desire to flee, I will not be able merely by willing myself to fight to override the desire to flee. So I must first will to change my bodily state, to get it to calm down and shape up, and then my body will affect the pineal gland in such a way as to cause it to give rise to the passion of courage in my mind, and the resultant bodily desire to fight. That is, merely willing according to the mind's reasoned desire to do something is inadequate; the body must be in a condition to carry out the desired action. In effect, for the mind successfully to will a bodily action, not only must there be a mental desire to do it, but also there must be a bodily desire to do it, and these desires in tandem trigger the will to satisfy them.

People with strong minds can alter their bodily motions so as to change their passions and bodily desires radically, but people with weak minds are very seldom able to overcome their initial bodily motions, passions, and bodily desires. The most effective actors are those who can control their bodies in such a way as to generate passions that cause bodily desires congruent with the desires of reason. And, as Descartes indicates, it is easier to work on bodily motions piecemeal by breaking them down into their component parts and changing them one at a time, e.g., to concentrate on changing trembling to calmness until one's body is fully ready for the action desired, rather than to try to force one's body outright to do what it is not prepared to do.

It is clear from the foregoing that the will is not itself a self-motivating power. It is an active power in that it initiates body movements (within physiological possibility). But it is itself activated by bodily desires that originate from passions caused by bodily movements. When Descartes talks of a strong will, what he actually means is a mind that is strong in the sense that it can often overcome the influence of natural passions and bodily desires. Someone said to have a weak will actually has a mind incapable of altering very many of its natural passions and bodily desires. But by adopting Descartes's method of breaking problems down to their elements, even a weak mind can alter its bodily motions (and thus its passions and bodily desires) by concentrating step-by-step on one small part of its bodily motions at a time.

C. Willing the Good

Because the human will is like the will of God, it has to be equally strong and neutral in everyone. Thus when Descartes says that "the will tends only toward objects that have some semblance of goodness" (CSM I 391; AT XI 464), he must mean that the soul has this tendency. It is the tendency of the soul to seek what its reason represents to it as good. Some souls have a weaker tendency to seek the good than others, but Descartes says that "Even those who have the weakest souls could acquire absolute mastery over all their passions if we employed sufficient ingenuity in training and guiding them" (CSM I 348; AT XI 370). As already indicated, it is clear that Descartes believes that the way to help people to do this is to teach them the rules of his method as expounded in the *Discours de la Méthode*. Step-by-step behavior modification is the way to overcome fear, e.g., of going into battle. First you learn to remain calm behind the lines, then right at the edge of a battle, then in the midst of a battle where you are relatively safe and not fighting, and finally as a participant. With the Cartesian method of controlling the passions, you can train yourself even to want to go into battle.

This method is used today by behavioral therapists to overcome phobias. For example, if you are afraid to use an elevator, you are first taken to stand and watch people getting into and out of an elevator. In the next session, you get into the elevator yourself to get used to it, but you don't go up or down. The next session, you go up one floor. And so on until you have trained your body not to make you afraid, even if you take an elevator to the top of the Empire State Building. Piecemeal conditioning is the key to training the will to control the body.

But the difficulty in stiffening even strong souls stems from the fact that "All the conflicts usually supposed to occur between the lower part of the soul that we call 'sensitive' and the higher or 'rational' part of the soul – or between the natural appetites [bodily desires] and the will [Descartes means "reason" here] – consist simply in the opposition between the movements that the body (by means of its will) tends to produce at the same time in the [pineal] gland" (CSM I 345–346; AT XI 364). Thus, "It is to the body alone [that gives rise to natural passions and bodily desires] that we should attribute everything that can be observed in us to oppose our reason" (CSM I 346; AT XI 365). Nevertheless, "there is within us but one soul, and this soul has within it no diversity of parts; it is at once sensitive and rational too, and all its appetites [desires raised by bodily motions] are [i.e., lead to] volitions" (CSM I 346; AT XI 364). Thus, the conflict itself takes place in the mind, and is not between conflicting volitions per se, but is between volitions instigated by desires of reason and volitions instigated by bodily desires. Volitions triggered by bodily desires derived from the passions conflict with volitions triggered by rational desires derived from the reason. The conflict of will in man – whom God has created through the union of body and mind – is really between the body and the mind.

The passions and the desires they raise "are all ordained by nature to relate to the body, and to belong to the soul only insofar as it is joined with the body. Hence, their natural function is to move the soul to consent and contribute to actions that may serve to preserve the body or render it in some way more perfect" (CSM I 376; AT XI 430). Thus the will is impelled to act mostly by the body. And when Descartes says of a person that he knows "that nothing truly belongs to him but this freedom to

dispose his volitions" (CSM I 384; AT XI 446), he must be thinking that the body is a temporary possession until death, and the
soul is permanent. If it were not for this linkage of the soul with
the body, the infinite will might never be impelled to exceed
understanding nor to choose the bad over the good, for there
would be no desire or need to do so. That is, without a body to
preserve in immediate action, there would be no impulsion to
make choices based on less than certain and complete knowledge. Thus, although Descartes says that "the soul can have
pleasures of its own," he goes on to say that "the pleasures common to it and the body depend entirely on the passions" (CSM
I 404; AT XI 488). It follows that "the chief use of wisdom lies in
its teaching us to be masters of our passions and to control them
with such skill that the evils that they cause are quite bearable,
and even become a source of joy" (CSM I 404; AT XI 488).

In the dual substance, man, the will automatically follows the
bodily desires, and if reason wants to alter bodily action, it must
alter the bodily motions that control the passions that give rise
to the desires that control the will.

Descartes's doctrine of the will, then, does not involve direct
control of gross bodily motions. The key requirement in this
mechanism is that the reason must have enough force to alter
the motions in the pineal gland so that the bodily behavior that
gives rise to a passion and resultant bodily desire that reason
does not desire is changed to bodily behavior that gives rise to
a passion and resultant bodily desire that reason does desire.

Descartes's doctrine of the will and its control is an expedi-
ent required by the union of the soul with the body. If the soul
were not united with a body that had to be protected, then there
would be no need for passions that arouse bodily desires that
incite "actions that may serve to preserve the body" (CSM I
376; AT XI 430). There would be no incentive or desire for the
will to exceed the understanding in a soul not united with a
body, and thus as the will – or the whole soul – tends toward the
good, there would be no need to control the will.

In an unembodied soul, volitions would automatically follow reason with no intervening passions or bodily desires. For non-human animals, on the other hand, bodily responses follow bodily stimulae with no intervening passions or bodily desires. This is because nonhuman animals do not have souls, and so they cannot have mental feelings such as passions and bodily desires. If the human body were not united to the soul, the will would play no role in bodily behavior at all; bodily reaction would follow bodily stimulus without any volitions taking place, just as in nonhuman animals. Again in parallel, in a soul not united to a body, volitions would be made for the good automatically without any deliberations taking place. The will, then, is a faculty needed by and operational in man alone. Only a being that consists of a union of a body and a rational soul in conflict needs to have a will. Only in man does the reason deliberate whether or not to follow bodily desires. This points up the fact that will belongs only to the mind; only self-conscious entities can will; willing is an intentional act.

Of course the entire human mechanism – of passions generated by the interaction of the body with material things, leading to bodily desires that incite volitions to bodily actions that protect the body – is required if the body is to preserve itself. But all of this could take place in the body – as it does according to Descartes in nonhuman animals – without union with a soul. In the case of animals, there are no volitions because animals are mere stimulus-response machines that do not have minds and thus no reason and no will.

That we do have wills can get us into trouble, because we may will to do something on the basis of inadequate knowledge. This never happens with animals, because they do not have understandings and so do not know anything. Their bodies simply respond to immediate material stimuli, although of course they can learn – their bodies are altered through experience – and their behavior can alter through time as they succeed in satisfying some desires and fail in satisfying others.

The pineal gland is the contact point between mind and body. Descartes's doctrine of the will is to the effect that a mental desire of reason can trigger the willing of micro-motions in the material pineal gland. These in turn cause changes in gross bodily behavior that result in a different bodily passion and resulting bodily desire. This new bodily desire then gives rise to a new passion that leads to a new volition that causes the gross bodily behavior that reason desires. So the soul must be able by will power to effect direct change in the motions of the pineal gland that in turn cause gross bodily motions.

Willings, i.e., volitions, can initiate bodily motion. Both bodily desires and desires of reason can trigger volitions. Thus, Descartes asserts that desires of the reason can direct the will immediately, just as can desires of the passions. When reason and the passions are in conflict, the desires of one must override the desires of the other to gain control of the will, and thus direct the micro-motions of the pineal gland.

Unfortunately, the battle between the passions and reason is strongly tipped in favor of the passions, for the natural response of the pineal gland is to cause the body to act to satisfy immediate bodily desires. Willing to satisfy immediate bodily desires merely reinforces the responses of the pineal gland that would occur naturally.

Further, it is predetermined which is the stronger. That is, the given nature of the mind and the given nature of the body determine which volitions – those from the reason or those from the passions – will dominate when in conflict. Both body and mind (reason) are finite; which is stronger depends on our natural constitutions that differ by birth in different men. Even so, Descartes teaches that reason can ultimately triumph over the passions in anyone, because we can outsmart the body by altering its motions bit-by-bit until it is in a state that causes us to have the passions and bodily desires that our reason has decided are best.

Descartes says that the passions are for the purpose of preserving the body, which is why, in the union of mind and body, body gains the greater advantage. A soul is likely to sin by giving in to some of the bodily passions, but the chances of a body's survival are enhanced by the help of reason. In particular, knowledge of medicine leads us to will to pursue some pains that we would otherwise flee, and to flee some pleasure that we would otherwise pursue, to the advantage of our bodily health.

Through control of passions that would otherwise run rampant, we can also pursue higher goals of civility, statecraft, military glory, and science. Perhaps most importantly, our possession of will and understanding – our being souls – makes us moral entities. Animals do not know the difference between good and bad, they do not choose one or the other, and hence they cannot be morally praised or blamed. It is our glory to be created in the image of God's infinite will, so that we have the power to choose between good and bad. Our freedom to err and to sin is what makes us moral beings. And it is union with the body that gives us this chance, for a disembodied soul neither would or could judge beyond knowledge or prefer the bad over the good. It is not even clear that there would be any purpose in a disembodied soul's having a will. What would it need it for?

On the other hand as a man – as a union of body and soul – is it even possible for me to be good? The answer to this question depends on the nature of and the relations between the two parts – the soul and the body – of the compound substance, man. As for the soul, Descartes assumes that all souls desire the good. They seek the good to the limit of their understanding, which has greater and smaller breadth and depth in different individuals (both in ultimate capacity and in content at a given time), but they can be misled by limited knowledge (which also includes misinformation and poor reasoning). But no matter how limited or weak the understanding may be, the soul still tends toward the good.

The agony and the ecstasy are always with the body. For it seems that without the body, a soul would be no more a moral being than is a non-human animal body machine. Just as mind-less animals are neither good nor bad because they must do what they do mechanically (and do not know they are doing it), it would seem also that an unembodied soul's natural tendency always toward the good without any bodily resistance would equally disqualify it as a moral agent that is good or bad because there is no way it could or would choose to do bad.

The crucial question of will power and morality, then, concerns embodied souls. How tractable is a human body to willful control? There is great variation among people. A body with a pineal gland particularly unsusceptible to volitions initiated by the reason might resist the attempts of the soul to which it is united to such a degree that the soul could not gain control of its passions. A soul united to such a strong or irrepressible body would not be able to override pineal-gland responses to volitions initiated by bodily desires, and thus could not change the passions. Would it be possible then for a soul united to such an unmalleable body to accept its passions and bear "the evils that they cause" (CSM I 404; AT XI 488)? Perhaps such a soul in union with such a body would comment on the way to the execution chamber, "I was born to be bad." Descartes would say that if such a soul went on to say, "And I deserve to die," such acceptance is a rational response to behavior caused by very strong passions. And he remarks on how obstinate some bodies are, so you might expect him to admit that it is impossible for some people to overcome their passions either by themselves or with community help. For example, in a letter defending a peasant who had killed his stepfather because he beat the young man's mother and was threatening to kill his brother, Descartes says that "all the movements of our passion not always being in our power, it sometimes happens that the best men commit very great faults" (AT IV 783).

But in *Les Passions de l'Âme*, Descartes in fact denies that any passions are uncontrollable. I have already quoted his comment that "Even those who have the weakest souls could acquire

absolute mastery over all their passions if we employed sufficient ingenuity in training and guiding them" (CSM I 348; AT XI
370). No body is so intractable that its passions cannot be controlled. The weakness of the soul here has to be not in will
power but in understanding and knowledge, for all wills are
equally infinite. So again, what is meant is not weakness of will,
but merely stubbornness of body and lack of knowledge how to
control it. Descartes says that animal trainers "are able, with a
little effort, to change the movements of the brain in animals
devoid of reason" (CSM I 348; AT XI 370), so we who have reason ought to be able to train our own bodies. It may take the
help of others, but because all souls tend toward the good and
want to be able to control bodily passions so bodily desires lead
to the willing of good actions, anybody can – and should – be so
guided.

Such could be the mechanistic theory behind monastic dis-
cipline and brainwashing. It certainly provides ground for the
practice suggested by Pascal to those who – like himself – want
to believe in Christianity but are plagued with doubt: Behave
like a believer and in time your belief will be generated from
your bodily actions. So you are an atheist? Go to Mass every
morning, say your prayers, confess, take communion – and one
day you will believe. Of course the major uses of these methods
in the 20th century have been by secular totalitarian govern-
ments, not to mention the repetitive techniques of modern
advertising.

D. The Sources of Willing

In conclusion, what I will depends on two sources. To the extent
that I am a soul that tends toward the good, I will what I think
to be good in the light of my limited understanding and knowledge. To the extent that I am a body that tends toward self-
preservation, I will to satisfy my bodily desires. As a being that
is a union of body and soul, I sometimes know that my body can
be better preserved if I overcome the responses to my initial

bodily desires, and sometimes I can substitute bodily actions and reactions that are better than the natural ones. And I also know that overcoming some of my initial bodily desires is necessary if I am to substitute morally good for bad behavior. I am always completely free to will any bodily action. Some bodily actions I cannot do because they are physically impossible. Whether or not I can effect those actions that are physically possible depends primarily on how coarsely or finely tuned my body and my pineal gland are to my will, and secondarily on the extent to which others help me to train my body should it be particularly recalcitrant to the control of my reason.

In sum, having an infinite will, an infinite power of will, or complete freedom of the will, which are three ways of saying the same thing, is far from having what is conventionally known as a strong will, a firm will, or great will power, which also are three ways of saying the same thing. For Descartes, all wills in themselves are unlimited in scope. All volitions are without degree, i.e., there are no degrees of willing, either one wills or does not: my volitions are no less volitions than are God's. But the will is not a self-activated power of the soul. The will is an active power of the soul that is triggered by desires generated either by the reason or by the body. Our bodily desires are sometimes not for the best because our bodies are not perfect. And our rational desires are sometimes wrongly directed because our souls have finite reason, limited understanding, and restricted knowledge. Even when we will for the best, we may not attain the good because our souls are united to bodies that are more or less susceptible to mental control. In the end, then, it is the nature of the body – its physical capacities and its atunement with the soul – that makes the difference between those we separate conventionally as either strong or weak willed.

Chapter 5

DID DESCARTES READ CORNEILLE?

Le Cid by Pierre Corneille (1606–1684) (Descartes was born in 1596) was published and performed in Paris in 1636. Descartes's *Discours de la Méthode* was published in Leiden in 1637. From 1629 through 1650 (the year of Descartes's death), Corneille presented at least ten major plays, most of which Descartes must have known about, and some of which he surely saw or read. There is, however, no direct evidence that Descartes knew of Corneille, nor Corneille of Descartes. Probably Descartes discussed Corneille with Princess Elisabeth, who in her youth performed in Corneille's comedy, *Médée* (1634) (AT XII 403–404). *Le Cid* was performed in The Hague in 1638 while Descartes was in The Netherlands, and Descartes's major publisher in The Netherlands, Louis Elzevier, printed twelve editions of Corneille's plays between 1641 and 1647 (AT XII 505–506). During those years, Elzevier printed at least seven items for Descartes, including editions of the *Meditations* and the *Principia*. Nevertheless, Adam says that "One cannot be assured, however, either that Descartes read Corneille, or that Corneille read Descartes. We know only that Corneille was well known in Holland" (AT XII 505).

Gustave Lanson agrees with Adam, despite the fact that "there is not merely an analogy, but an identity of spirit in the

Les Passions de l'Âme and Corneillian tragedy."[1] To show this, Lanson cites heroes of the will from Corneille, e.g., Auguste in *Cinna*: "I am master of myself as of the universe. I am such as I will to be." And he quotes Pauline in *Polyeucte*: "And on my passions my reason is sovereign."

Lanson follows this with citations from Descartes's *Les Passions de l'Ame*:

> Article 40. – That there is no soul so feeble that it cannot, when well conducted, acquire an absolute power over its passions.

> Article 41. – . . . The will is so free by its nature that it can never be restrained.[2]

Descartes goes on in the *Passions* to show how one can overcome unwanted passions, such as fear, by representing to oneself the glory that would come from being courageous, with the result that courage is substituted for fear. Corneille's heroes reason with themselves in the same way, representing to themselves the good effects of having certain passions, in order to overcome destructive and unworthy passions. In both cases reason is and ought to be master of the passions.

This is cold-blooded reasoning. As Lanson says, "the Corneillean heroes are always *conscious* and always *reasoners*: they form *firm and determined judgments* to support their will, the spring of their action."[3] The worst sort of weak-willed character for both Descartes and Corneille is someone who acts on impulse. The name of the game for them is control: one must choose one's passions; whom one loves and whom one hates must be a matter of reason, not of sentiment. Thus, in *Rodogune*, Emilie hates Auguste because she thinks him a tyrant, but when he shows himself to be generous, she reasons that she should love him. In the play, the change is breathtaking: "My hate that I believed immortal is going to die. It is dead."[4]

In particular, Lanson stresses those passages in which both Descartes and Corneille insist that they can be masters of themselves, and thereby masters of the universe. The goal of calculated reason is goodness, virtue, and perfection. As long as you are modest and generous in the sense of recognizing your own material and mental limitations, and as long as you follow your reason, you can be satisfied that you are virtuous.

If there were any direct influence between the two, it would be from Corneille to Descartes. As Lanson points out, *Les Passions de l'Ame* was written in 1646 and published in 1649, and by then most of Corneille's main works had appeared.[5] On the other hand, Lanson says "I find in the *Treatise [on the Passions]* Nicomède as well as Auguste; and Nicomède is posterior to 1649."[6] Lanson concludes from this:

> Therefore, there was no influence of the one on the other, but rather community of inspiration.
> Both the philosopher and the poet have worked on the same model: the man that French society commonly presented at the beginning of the 17th century. . . . The race formed by the disorders and perils of the 16th century is robust, intelligent, and active. It has brutal senses; a mind that is quick, supple, lucid, and practical; and a sound and intact will. Between the appetites of the senses and the ideas of the mind, no place is left for the pure emotions of the heart or the soft reveries of the imagination. It lives both physical life and intellectual life with intensity, and has no sentimental life whatsoever. Above all it esteems clear judgments and prompt decisions. Its ideal is always to keep all the forces of its body and soul under command. . . . Look at Richelieu, Retz, Turenne, Bussy . . . the domination of intelligence and of the will in Richelieu . . . solid men, strongly sensual but not at all sensitive, intellectuals who transform their impressions into ideas, their ideas into judgments, their judgments into acts of will, who know what they want, want what they are, and for whom life is entire-

ly a work of clear conscience and free determination
– if one understands by freedom solely the power of
pure ideas to determine one's acts.[7]

Cassirer agrees with Lanson about the lack of mutual influence between Descartes and Corneille. But he stresses even
further the likeness between them. The ideal man for both
Descartes and Corneille has "a fixed and immutable center,"[8]
with a stringently restricted character. In particular, Descartes's
man in control of his passions and Corneille's plays, and the
characters in them, behave like clockwork machines:

> All their movements can be foreseen by calculations.
> Once the particular springs that move the men of
> Corneille are given, and once the particular "charac-
> ter" each of them embodies in the drama is given,
> then the totality of their actions and reactions is there-
> by already given. We see how they work just as we
> see the inside of a clock: once set in motion, the
> mechanism of the clock will always take the same
> determined course. For Corneille, everything obeys
> the laws of a mechanics of the passions, laws that
> admit of no exception. Once the forces by which men
> are animated are given, their effects are thereby
> given.[9]

The details of this mechanism of the passions are worked out in
Descartes's *Les Passions de l'Ame.*

In particular, both Corneille and Descartes stress that one
should observe oneself with detachment in order to analyze
one's passions and to make judgments about one's actions. The
will always is presented as following judgment concerning the
passions. In this way the spiritual nature of the soul triumphs
over the material nature of the body.[10]

Cassirer quotes from Descartes's first letter (of 20
November 1647) to Queen Christina that "Free will is in itself

the most noble thing that could be in us because it makes us in some way like God and seems to exempt us from being his subjects"[11] (AT V 85). This will is the central power of the self-conscious soul, but it is controlled by the reason in the light of knowledge of the physiological causes of our passions. To know the causes of our passions is to be able to control them. For both Descartes and Corneille, the overriding reasons for altering the passions stem from the code of the gentleman. Truth and goodness, honor and virtue, temperance and reason – these stand against mere bodily passions and desires.

Both Descartes and Corneille center the character of man – and of woman – in a strong will. The major difference between Descartes's and Corneille's doctrines of the will is that Descartes gives guidance for how to contend with one's desires in the struggle to follow reason, while Corneille's heroes often change instantly with no struggle at all from following their desires to doing what honor demands. On the other hand, Descartes considers all of humankind, whereas Corneille's heroes and heroines are taken from the noble classes, whose bodily natures (Descartes agrees) are more highly attuned to reason than those of common folk.

Of course one can get in trouble with a strong will. Both Descartes and Corneille face the possibility of erring when a strong will is employed to make a choice in action with limited understanding and knowledge. Any choice made in light of one's full knowledge, they believe, is of the highest value even when wrong. As long as one has resolved to do good, one's willed actions cannot be morally faulted, even though they might be disastrous. This is the soul of tragedy.

Cassirer extends this view into the doctrine that pure intensity of will has moral value independent of the moral value of the goal striven for.[12] Cassirer accounts for both Descartes and Corneille adhering to this opinion by saying that "The 16th and 17th centuries in the domain of moral philosophy are characterized by a *renaissance of Stoicism*."[13] But the tranquility of soul

that is to result is far from being one of resignation. Both
Descartes and Corneille profess "a radically active Stoicism,"[14]
so that one's contentment and satisfaction are in doing the best
one can. Cassirer says that "The goal and ambition of
Corneillean tragedy is to awaken similar passions, and not pure-
ly irrational instincts. It is in this that the spirit of French
Classicism is closely allied to the spirit of Cartesian philosophy."[15]

Cornelia Serrurier also claims that there was no direct influence between Descartes and Corneille, but that they were inde-
pendently influenced by reading Saint François de Sales's *Traité
de l'Amour de Dieu* published in 1616.[16] She doubts that
Descartes and Corneille got their models from the great men of
their day, saying, "What an abyss between the character, e.g., of
the Cid and that of the cruel Richelieu, and between the *generous man* of Descartes and the vile schemer de Retz."[17] Instead,
she quotes passage after passage, first from Saint François de
Sales's *Traité de l'Amour de Dieu,* and then from Descartes and
Corneille. Reason over the passions, control of the passions by
the will, and the love of virtue, all of these combine in the three
authors. When the *Traité de l'Amour de Dieu* appeared,
Descartes was twenty and Corneille was ten. Serrurier says it is
virtually certain that a book of such renown was read by
Descartes on his own and was assigned to Corneille by his
Jesuit teachers. (Both Descartes and Corneille went to the
Jesuit college in La Flèche, although Corneille was there ten
years after Descartes.) And in Saint François de Sales's *Traité,*
Serrurier says that

> Before Descartes and Corneille, Saint François had
> shown that the will, enlightened by the reason, has
> the power to force love, to attach itself to the true
> good, and to turn itself away from a formerly desired
> false good. *The will can reject its love by applying the
> understanding to the motives that disgust it.* This is a

thought of Saint François de Sales that is found near-
ly word-for-word in the *Treatise on the Passions of the
Soul* of Descartes and that the heroes of the
Corneillean theatre put in practice.[18]

All three were trained by the Jesuits, and as Serrurier says,
"Theories glorifying the power of a good will were dear to the
Jesuits of the epoch."[19] The doctrine of an active will was posed
against the passive fatalism of Calvin and Jansen.

I agree with Serrurier that it is most unlikely that Descartes
and Corneille were not influenced by the Jesuits and by Saint
François de Sales. By the same arguments, it is most unlikely
that they did not read and influence each other.

Robert Champigny tries to show that there is a real difference between Descartes's men of will and Corneille's heroes.[20]
But the difference, it seems to me from the passages
Champigny quotes and the examples he gives, is mostly one of
contrast within a system that puts will or reason in conflict with
the passions. As Champigny says, for Descartes, "The soul does
not have passions, it suffers them,"[21] and thus "The conflict
between will and passion takes place between the soul and the
body."[22] Champigny does not work this out in detail as I do
above, but instead goes on to argue that while Descartes recognizes that the blind passions are always with us even when we
overcome them, Corneille seems to think that we can excise
unwanted passions entirely.[23] I agree that it would be pretty
absurd of Corneille to think this, and see the claim that he does
as a moot point in Corneillean scholarship. On the other hand,
Champigny's conclusion that Corneille gives a psychologically
accurate picture of fanaticism does not seem to me, as it does to
him, to be an argument against the congruence of Corneillean
and Cartesian heroes. I wonder if anyone other than a fanatic
could maintain such powerful control of the will as Descartes
advocates. And finally, I think Champigny chooses a particularly unfortunate metaphor with which to close his argument. He

says that "Philosophy and the theatre are enemies" and then goes on to explain that "The mission of the philosopher is to tear off the masks. Now precisely behind the masks is where the theatre lives, whether on the stage or in the street."[24] But a major problem in Cartesian scholarship just is that Descartes is the man in the mask.

In his exhaustive study "The Place of Poetry in Descartes' Life and Background," William McC. Stewart quotes Descartes from the *Discours* as saying that he "actually *was in love with poetry*" (CSM I 114; AT VI 7).[25] It is clear that Descartes did read and appreciate poetry, and certainly wrote verses in Latin in his youth as did all the students at La Flèche. Stewart stresses both Descartes's literary bent and his probable opinion of the use of poetry by commenting that

> In a Latin letter in the style of Petronius written in 1628 in defense of his friend Guez de Balzac [a literary stylist], creative use is undoubtedly made [by Descartes], as it seems to us, of a vivid recollection of a famous passage of the *Epistle ad Pisones (Ars poetica)* in which Horace glorifies the civilizing force of poetry.[26]

Stewart also points out that Descartes had to have been quite familiar with the *Corpus Poetarum*, a compendium of literally all of Latin poetry, that figures so prominently in one of Descartes's dreams of 10 November 1619. Stewart says

> This *Corpus Poetarum* is interpreted by [Descartes] as signifying "Philosophy and wisdom joined together." It lies open in his dream at the page with the words "Quod vitae sectabor iter?" [What course of life should I take?] and these are in fact the opening words of the Idyll of Ausonius classed as fifteenth in the volume in question. At the same time, in his dream, an unknown man presents him with a piece of

verse: the words "Est et Non" [Yes and No] catch his eye. Now these are in fact the opening words of the Idyll of Ausonius classed in the *Corpus* as seventeenth and to be found in the second column of the same page of the volume.[27]

These verses of Ausonius have to do with what choices one should make in life, and out of the dreams Descartes makes his, significantly not for poetry, but for science. Stewart goes on to say that "Descartes proceeds, in the *Discours*, to tell us that he thought that both eloquence and poetry were natural gifts *(des dons de l'esprit)* rather than fruits of study."[28] Descartes doubtless knew where his own talents lay.

The only novel Descartes is known to have read is *Amadis de Gaul*, an immense epic of chivalry, which he apparently read more than once. It is probable that Descartes acted in at least one play at La Flèche, and, as remarked, wrote poetry there.[29] He knew drama as well as poetry, and as Stewart points out, "Many of the examples found in his work are drawn from the drama."[30] It would not be mistaken to say that in some sense Descartes viewed life as theater. For example, in a letter written in January, 1646, to Princess Elisabeth to counsel her on her depression, Descartes says that one ought not allow "the troubles that come to us from outside, no matter how great they are, to enter into our minds any farther than the sadness caused by actors when they represent very distressing actions in front of us" (AT IV 355).

Descartes's *La Recherche de la Verité par la Lumiere Naturelle* was probably written in 1641, and was not published in his lifetime. It is an unfinished dialogue, and is not a literary success.

Descartes apparently did try his hand at theater at some point in his life, as he is said to have finished at least three acts of a comedy. Stewart quotes from Leibniz's notes about this work that it had "the air of a pastoral or a rustic fable."[31] Leibniz found it to be a strange play. It starts traditionally with Alixan and Parthenis each believing the other to be a peasant, although each is the child of a prince. Then in the very first act (instead of the last as is conventional), Alixan overhears Parthenis debating with herself whether or not she, a princess, should love Alixan, a peasant. She decides that she should love him, and on the spot Alixan comes forth from his hiding place and declares himself to be a prince. It is difficult to imagine how the rest of the play would then go, and Leibniz does not say. The only thing we do know about the play, however, is very Corneillean: Parthenis reasons that because of Alixan's virtue, she should love him even though he is a peasant, and does so. As befits the abruptness of the Corneillean treatment of the passions, she is immediately rewarded by Parthenis revealing himself to be a prince.

Descartes may have written this play when he was friends with Guez de Balzac and perhaps other literary figures in Paris in his youth. No copy is known to have survived.

The best evidence that Descartes knew Corneille's work is that his close friend and frequent correspondent Constantijn Huygens, who lived in The Hague, wrote two verses as introduction to the edition of Corneille's *Le Menteur* [*The Liar*] that Louis Elzevier published in Leiden in 1645. Corneille reproduced Huygens' verses in the 1648 Paris edition, and the two corresponded in 1649 and 1650. In 1650, Corneille dedicated his *Don Sanche d'Aragon* to Huygens (AT V 591–592).

Costabel remarks that

> By a curious coincidence that is perhaps relevant, the "Liar" of Corneille's comedy is a young student freshly debarked from Paris who comes to Poitiers, the university renowned for studies in law. Now Descartes was a Poitvian and it is precisely at Poitiers that he earned his degrees of Bacheler and Licentee in 1616. He also quickly quit the robe for the sword, and as Corneille says, "put bankrupt to this balderdash of laws" (AT V 592).

As the epigraph to this present work indicates, Huygens sent verses to Descartes, and they must have discussed poetry. Descartes surely would have known Corneille's works at least through Huygens.

Adam provides further circumstantial evidence. He remarks that *Le Cid* was published in Leiden by Louis Elzevier in 1638:

> The Elzeviers printed *Le Cid* again in 1641 and 1644; *Horace* in 1641, 1645, 1647; *Cinna* in 1644 and 1648; *Polyeucte* the same dates; *L'Illustre Théâtre* in 1644, in which were bound in one volume the five preceding plays; *Le Menteur* and *La Suite du Menteur*, 1645 and 1647; *Rodogune*, 1647. (AT XII 506)

Also, as mentioned above, Corneille's comedy *Médée* was put on at the Palatine court in The Hague in 1641 or 1642 by the young princesses of the court. Princess Sophie played the role of Nérine. Descartes's friend and correspondent Princess Elisabeth acted in the play, too, but which role is not known (AT XII 506). As the eldest sister in a family performance, perhaps she played the enchantress Medea (a role, by the way, perhaps better fitted to Queen Christina). Huygens, who was in close touch with Descartes at this time, could have seen this performance. For that matter, Descartes could have been there. In his correspondence with Princess Elisabeth, the first extant letter of 6 May 1643 indicates that she and Descartes already knew each other well (AT XII 403).

Recently, Jean-Marie Beyssade has made an exhaustive comparison of the writings of Descartes and Corneille.[32] He exhibits many parallels, but does not venture any comment concerning the possible influence of either one upon the other. But did Corneille read Descartes and did Descartes read Corneille? Of course they did. And did they influence one another? Of course they did. There is no direct evidence of it, but two elephants dancing in the same ring cannot avoid bumping into one another.

Chapter 6

DESCARTES'S POLITICAL PHILOSOPHY

A. Evidence and Methods of Construction

To justify my claim that Descartes has a political philosophy, I use a contextual method. First I present some facts about Descartes's life, then I use these facts to discuss Descartes's politics. Descartes politics is the foundation on which I construct his political philosophy.

But going from Descartes's background and behavior to his politics is far from enough. My next step is to focus heavily on Descartes's code of conduct in the *Discours de la Méthode* (1637). There are logical connections between this code and some parts of Descartes's political philosophy. This is true also for the constitution he wrote for Queen Christina's proposed Swedish Academy of Arts and Sciences, and for the program he is said to have devised for a state-supported School of Arts and Crafts in Paris. Both of these institutions were established after his death.

Then it gets more complicated. For deriving points of Descartes's political philosophy from *Les Passions de l'Âme* (1649), both the circumstances of its composition and publication, and the logical implications of its doctrine of the will are important. The situation is difficult in another way concerning the other work Descartes is purported to have published in 1649, *La Naissance de la Paix.* I have already discounted this ballet as a source of Descartes's political philosophy

My methodological argument, then, is this: The picture of Descartes's political philosophy that I present here is supported by logical inferences from what he says in various texts. But this is not enough to make the claim that it is Descartes's political philosophy and not just a Cartesian political philosophy. Beyond making these logical inferences, I argue that Descartes himself did or would have made them.

B. The Sovereign

Descartes never wrote systematically on political philosophy, nor did he ever express any interest in presenting one. It is not surprising, then, that few people have ever suggested that he had one. Now I believe that Descartes's political views have in fact had an influence in Western philosophy, particuarly his individualism, which he stresses despite his championing of monarchy. But if Descartes did have a political philosophy, it is scattered in fragments throughout his works. Thus I construct a political philosophy for Descartes from these fragments.

Descartes was an advocate of monarchy, of an authoritarian royalist state in which the sovereign monarch's rule is invested by God. The sovereign appoints a court of advisors who meet in council with the sovereign in the chair. The advisors all speak in turn on each question before them, and discussion proceeds also in turn. Then the sovereign decides the question. All power resides in the sovereign, who is ultimately judge and legislator.

The sovereign is not a dictator. Descartes's ideal state is not an absolutism of the totalitarian sort. But it is certainly an authoritarian monarchy, not a democracy. Whatever the God-fearing king does is right, but he does not make the Truth. Sometimes to protect the unity of the state, the king can lie. But as a philosopher, Descartes's problem is to reconcile truth and authority. He must compromise, as any political philosopher must. Revolution and anarchy are worse than absolutism, even if it is misused. But, just as the king should not try to impose his regime's morality and beliefs on other peoples, and thus should be tolerant of them, he should practice tolerance and discretion at home for the good of his own people.[1]

The sovereign is commander in chief of the military and titular head of the state church, but in practice he delegates the duties and authority of these offices to appointees who supervise the hierarchically organized members of these institutions. Both the military and the church defend and uphold the state.

Besides controlling revenues from state property and lands, of which he is virtual owner to do with as he pleases, the sovereign invests a revenue department with the authority to collect taxes.

The sovereign's near peers are the noble landowners, who have sworn loyalty to the crown, which they can be called upon to defend. In return, they are given grants of money, income from properties, and are relieved of taxes. On the other hand, their money, property, and land are subject to seizure by the crown, even though Descartes believed that a strong noble class strengthens the state and the crown.

Descartes further believed that the state religion should be that which is traditional to the state. This could be either Catholic or Protestant in Europe, Muslim farther east, and Confucian or otherwise even farther east. And although the state religion is dominant, other religions are tolerated as long as they do not foment insurrection. In particular, Protestants and Jews are to be tolerated in Catholic countries. Proselytizing and conversion are allowed, however, only by and to the state religion. In general, everyone should stick to the religion he was born and raised in.

States maintain their independence and status by military power. Peace among states is preferred, but when diplomacy fails, war is necessary. In fact, peace is almost always imposed by a powerful state that conquers other states. In such circumstances, the conquering state has the right to the spoils of war. Portable property such as art objects, gold, and jewelry appropriately accrue to the conquering sovereign; land and peoples can be annexed. In other words, imposed peace means an increase of the sovereign's power over conquered states and peoples. Peace is *kept* by the state.

Wars are not undertaken merely for conquest or to gain booty. A strong state does not have the right simply to build an empire out of weaker states or peoples. Again, war is justified only by the need and desire to impose peace.

The subjects of the state are divided into three classes, the aforementioned nobles, priests and judges, and commoners. All are citizens subject to calls to service by the crown. All are free to pursue their own interests as long as these are not subversive of the crown and state. This is particularly pertinent concerning Catholics, especially priests, whose loyalty to Rome cannot be allowed to override their loyalty to the state.

The state supports schools of which again the sovereign is titular head. These are men's academies under the direction of the state church, but they include non-clerical professors teaching such secular subjects as engineering, medicine, and military tactics. The schools are designed to accommodate the sons of all three classes. Although women are equal to men in nature and intelligence, schools for women are primarily religious. Exceptional women can be educated as men are, to become scholars and leaders. An important part of all education is the exposition of the operation of the passions and the training of the will to control and utilize the passions. Such reformative training is also carried on in prisons.

Although talented commoners are recognized and encouraged, the noble class is in fact of a higher order than commoners and those priests and judges who are not of the nobility. Nobles are more intelligent, more loyal, more sensitive, and more moral than other citizens. This is a sheer matter of birth.

To maintain this natural superiority, nobles should marry in their own ranks, or only among other citizens who have overcome the handicaps of their birth.

The state fosters free trade and encourages commerce. It institutes an academy of sciences, especially for engineering and medicine, with colleges open to the best practitioners in these areas. The state provides schools, tools, equipment, workplaces, and laboratories for artists, craftsmen, scientists, and scholars, and gives them annuities so that they can spend all their time working to improve the lot of mankind.

In sum, Descartes's political philosophy is in support of a benevolent despotism. States are ruled by hereditary monarchies. The crown is assisted by a minority class of nobles who are superior by birth and blood. Priests and judges are bound in service to the monarch. The majority class of commoners is in principle left as free as is consistent with state security, and is educated as much as is appropriate for the purpose of the advancement of commerce and industry.

The ideal goals of the state are three:

1. The imposition and maintenance of peace within the state and among states.

2. The enrichment of the state through commerce and industry.

3. The improvement of all mankind through the advancement of science – primarily physics and medicine – leading to the control of nature, which facilitates (1) and (2) above.

C. Descartes's Life and Politics

Descartes's father was a lawyer who had purchased a position as councilor in the legislature of Brittany, which made him a lowest-level member of the nobility, an ennoblement that would be hereditary only after the position had been held for three generations. And in fact this status was secured, because

Descartes's brother Pierre succeeded his father, and Pierre's son succeeded him. Descartes himself took degrees in canon and civil law in Poitiers in 1616. One of his maternal uncles, who was also his godfather, was in the court in Poitiers, and a total of at least nineteen of Descartes's uncles and cousins were lawyers in the service of the king.

Descartes's father sent him to La Flèche, Henry IV's new academy for training the sons of the realm to be of service to the crown. Descartes did well at school. After graduating from La Flèche and earning his law degrees in Poitiers, Descartes spent fifteen months in the service of Maurice, Prince of Nassau, in The Netherlands, learning to be a military engineer, but also learning Dutch and studying mathematics. Then he spent nine years traveling in Northern Europe, Italy, and France, again following the military and developing his mathematical method. Finally, in 1628, at the age of thirty-two, he moved permanently to The Netherlands, where he lived until about four months before his death in Sweden in 1650.

In The Netherlands, Descartes had a close intellectual and personal friendship with Princess Elisabeth of Bohemia. He wrote *Les Passions de l'Ame* at her request, although he later dedicated the published version in 1649 to Queen Christina of Sweden. In August of 1649, he dutifully heeded Queen Christina's call to her court, despite his judgment that going would destroy his health and tranquility, which it did.

One of the most tantalizing aspects of Descartes life is that he was raised among Protestants. He was born in La Haye, and was raised in Châtellerault until the age of ten. Both of these towns were designated as safe Protestant cities by the Edict of Nantes in 1598, two years after Descartes was born. There were large majorities of Protestants in this region. Then Descartes served under the Protestant Prince of Nassau. He lived most of his adult life in The Netherlands, a Protestant country, was the confidant of the Protestant Princess Elisabeth, and went when called to the court of the Protestant Queen Christina. Lest you suspect me of suggesting something here, let me quickly add that Descartes is said to have carried with him all his life his certificate of baptism in the Catholic Church, that he always tried to live near a Catholic community in The Netherlands where he could go to Mass, that he dedicated the *Meditations* to the Catholic theological faculty at the Sorbonne, and that when he was dying in Sweden he refused the attentions of a Protestant doctor, who he thought might poison him.

But The Netherlands was a republic, and given that Descartes lived there for twenty-two years, why isn't this evidence that his political philosophy is republican? Descartes certainly enjoyed the advantages of the most free state in Europe of his time. But there is nothing in his writings to support the view that he was a republican, and when he got into trouble with some Protestant ministers in The Netherlands, he ran to the French Ambassador and solicited the protection of the Prince of Nassau.

After Descartes died, Queen Christina wanted to bury him in the Protestant cemetery, but the French Ambassador Hector-Pierre Chanut – with whom Descartes was living in Stockholm – would not allow it. So Descartes was buried in unconsecrated ground reserved for unbaptized infants until his bones were removed to the Catholic soil of France.

Once when pressed to defend his religion, Descartes refused with the retort that he held the faith of his king and his nurse, and that this was his last and sufficient word on the subject.

Descartes was a royalist, a Catholic, and a traditionalist (today we would say he was a conservative). These were the politics to which he was loyal all his life. This can be derived from his life, but also from his code of conduct in the *Discours de la Méthode*, to which I now turn.

D. *Discours de la Méthode*

There is more of political interest in the *Discours* than the code of conduct, but let's look at it first.

It is commonplace today to assert that Descartes's first maxim is a foundation of conservatism. He vows

> to obey the laws and customs of my country, holding constantly to the religion in which by God's grace I had been instructed from my childhood, and governing myself in all other matters according to the most moderate and least extreme opinions – the opinions commonly accepted in practice by the most sensible of those with whom I should have to live. (CSM I 122; AT VI 23)

Descartes states this as part of "a provisional moral code" (CSM I 122; AT VI 22), but in asserting that "my whole aim was to reach certainty" (CSM I 125; AT VI 29), he explicitly excludes the moral code from contention, saying that "Once I had established these maxims and set them on one side together with the truths of faith, which have always been foremost among my beliefs, I judged that I could freely undertake to rid myself of all the rest of my opinions" (CSM I 125; AT VI 28).

But, and this is my arguing point, nowhere in any of his subsequent writings or behavior does he challenge or modify or give up his "provisional" moral code.

Descartes also provides a ground for the procedure I use above, that of deriving his politics from his behavior. He says he thought he ought to govern himself by following "the opinions most commonly accepted in practice by the most sensible of those with whom I should have to live," and he goes on to say that "in order to discover what opinions they really held I had to attend to what they did rather than what they said" (CSM I 122; AT VI 23).

Descartes reiterates his adherence to moderation, refining his principle by saying that "Where many opinions were equally well accepted, I chose only the most moderate, both because these are always the easiest to act upon and probably the best, all excess customarily being bad, and also so that if I made a mistake, I should depart less from the right path than I would if I chose one extreme when I ought to have pursued the other" (CSM I 122–123: AT VI 24).

Descartes's second maxim follows closely on the first. It is "to be as firm and decisive in my actions as I could, and to follow even the most doubtful opinions, once I had adopted them, with no less constancy than if they had been quite certain" (CSM I 123; AT VI 24). To indicate that I am not just using the negative evidence that Descartes never later challenges or revises these maxims, let me note that Descartes says that this second maxim about the necessity of making decisions on uncertain evidence is itself "true and certain." That is,

> *It is a most certain truth* that when it is not in our power to discern the truest opinions, we must follow the most probable. Even when no opinions appear more probable than any others, we must still adopt some; and having done so we must then regard them not as doubtful, from a practical point of view, but as most true and certain, *on the grounds that the reason which made us adopt them is itself true and certain.* (CSM I 123; AT VI 25)

So much for the provisionality of at least the second maxim in the moral code.

The third maxim is one of the most celebrated, having deep roots as it does in Descartes's mature metaphysical position concerning the relationship between the mind and the body detailed most concisely in *Les Passions de l'Ame*. Descartes resolves

> to try always to master myself rather than fortune, and change my desires rather than the order of the world. In general I would become accustomed to believing that nothing lies entirely within our power except our thoughts, so that after doing our best in

dealing with matters external to us, whatever we fail to achieve is absolutely impossible so far as we are concerned. (CSM I 123; AT VI 25)

Descartes really drives this point home, going on to say that "Making a virtue of necessity, as they say, we shall not desire to be healthy when ill or free when imprisoned, any more than we now desire to have bodies of a material as indestructible as diamonds or wings to fly like the birds" (CSM I 124; AT VI 26). It is very striking that both the second and the third maxims are meant by Descartes to free oneself from "the regrets and remorse that usually trouble the consciences of . . . weak and faltering spirits" (CSM I 123; AT VI 25).

The fourth maxim is merely Descartes's decision to "devote my whole life to cultivating my reason and advancing as far as I could in the knowledge of the truth, following the method I had prescribed for myself" (CSM I 124; AT VI 27). This method is not, by the way, his moral code, but rather his four-part method of investigation. That is, one should:

1. Accept as true only those things for which there is evidence of truth.

2. Divide problems into their smallest parts.

3. Order thoughts to move from simple to complex.

4. Make complete enumerations and comprehensive reviews of reasoning. (CSM I 120; AT VI 18–19)

But, as I say above, there is much more than a traditionalist or conservative code of conduct in the *Discours*. There is also ground for supporting the political philosophy of monarchy. Descartes says that "there is not usually so much perfection in works composed of several parts and produced by various different craftsmen as in the works of one man" (CSM I 116; AT VI 11), and goes on to provide an example of this by stating that "If Sparta was at one time very flourishing, this was not because each of its laws in particular was good . . , but because they were devised by a single man and hence all tended to the same end" (CSM I 117; AT VI 12).

Even before he states his first maxim about adhering to the laws, customs, and religion of one's own country, Descartes argues strenuously that "it would be unreasonable for an individual to plan to reform a state by changing it from the foundations up and overturning it in order to set it up again" (CSM I 117; AT VI 13). He makes clear that he is opposed to revolution, and even to reform, insisting on the excessive "difficulties . . . encountered in the reform even of minor matters affecting public institutions" (CSM I 117–118; AT VI 14). He goes on to explain that

> These large bodies are too difficult to raise up once overthrown, or even to hold up once they begin to totter, and their fall cannot but be a hard one. Moreover, any imperfections they may possess – and their very diversity suffices to ensure that many do possess them – have doubtless been much smoothed over by custom; and custom has even prevented or imperceptibly corrected many imperfections that prudence could not so well provide against. Finally, it is almost always easier to put up with their imperfections than to change them. (CSM I 118; AT VI 14)

Descartes supports this view with the analogy that it is better to follow an established winding road through the mountains than to set out on a direct route. This is in sharp contrast to the analogy Descartes provides to support his second maxim about making a choice and sticking with it. That is, when lost in a forest you should choose a direction and stay straight on it. If you have a road, follow it; but if you do not have a road, do not take the easiest turn at every juncture; instead go straight ahead whatever is in front of you.

Descartes's moral code is as much a foundation rock of his

metaphysics as the four-part method given above. This is shown when Descartes explains his fourth maxim, that is, his choice to cultivate his reason and seek truth, by saying that after all, "the sole basis of the foregoing three maxims was the plan I had to continue my self-instruction" (CSM I 124; AT VI 27). In a passage I quote above, Descartes explicitly excludes from any need of doubt or investigation "these maxims...together with the truths of faith" (CSM I 125; AT VI 28), and this in an endeavor in which he says that "my whole aim was to reach certainty" (CSM I 125; AT VI 29). It is not too much to insist, as I do, that the whole enterprise rests on his assurance of the truth and certainty of his method of investigation and of his code of conduct.

Descartes later insists on a similar exclusion or immunity when he is trying to defend himself from arguing in a circle or falling into complete doubt from which he cannot extricate himself in the First Meditation. In "Comments on a Certain Broadsheet," for example, Descartes says with wonderfully self-righteous huffiness, "What could be more perverse than to ascribe to a writer views that he reports simply in order to refute?" (CSM I 309; AT VIIIB 367). In the *Meditations*, he merely warns us; in the *Discours*, Descartes says outright that his scientific method, his moral code, and his religious faith are out of play – they are not susceptible to the skeptical criticism Descartes uses in the First Meditation to cast doubt on all other knowledge. Obviously, this mere assertion of immunity to skeptical doubt is not sufficient to protect these views from criticism, but that is another matter. Here, for present purposes, I take, as does Descartes, his provisional code as foundational, and I think I have presented enough to justify the obvious logical extensions from this code to the construction of major points in Descartes's political philosophy.

Three other extrapolations from the *Discours* can be quickly supported. On tolerance, Descartes says that "I have recognized through my travels that those with views quite contrary to ours are not on that account barbarians or savages, but that

many of them make use of reason as much or more than we do"
(CSM I 119; AT VI 16). He then goes on to say that because "it
is custom and example that persuade us [this, by the way, does
not go against his claim that his moral code is certain, because
it asserts the truth of the maxims, one of which is to follow local
customs, not the truth of the customs themselves], yet a majority vote is worthless as a proof of truths that are difficult to discover; for a single man is much more likely to hit upon them
than a group of people" (CSM I 119; AT VI 15), which I take to
lead directly to monarchy in opposition to democracy.

There is no question, however, that this monarchy is not
established for the benefit of the monarch, but for the people. In
Part VI of the *Discours*, Descartes makes his famous statement
that we are to learn to "know the power and action of fire, water,
air, the stars, the heavens, and all the other bodies in our envi-
ronment . . . and thus make ourselves, as it were, the lords and
masters of nature . . . and most importantly, for the maintenance
of health" (CSM I 142–143; AT VI 62). That this is a humanitarian goal, a project aimed at the good of the community as a
whole, is confirmed by his immediately prior statement that he
could not keep his discoveries of some "general notions in
physics . . . secret without sinning gravely against the law which
obliges us to do all in our power to secure the general welfare
of mankind" (CSM I 142; AT VI 61).

There is a natural reason for this humanitarianism in
Descartes. The survival and well being of the individual
depends on the survival and well being of the group. Descartes
states this explicitly in a letter of 15 September 1645 to
Elizabeth:

> Although each one of us is a person separate from all
> others, and by consequence everyone's interests are
> in some ways distinct from those of everyone else's,
> you should not think that you could live alone, for
> each of us is, in effect, one of the parts of the uni-
> verse, and even more particularly, one of the parts of

the earth, one of the parts of this state, of this society, of this family, to which one is joined by one's place
of residence, one's oath, and one's birth. Thus it is
always necessary to prefer the interests of the whole,
of which one is a part, to those of oneself in particular. (AT IV 290)

Descartes's political philosophy, then, is naturally, structurally,
and foundationally communal and humanitarian, even given
that the most important unit in society is the individual self-conscious human being. Each of us is to work for the good of the
community, which is to work for our own good.

Finally, in the *Discours*, there is a comment that stands to
Descartes's political philosophy not as a premise to a derived
conclusion but as a movement from experience to conviction,
and so leads again to the less-than-logical inference from his life
to his politics to his political philosophy of the sort I presented
prior to turning to the *Discours*. That is, Descartes says that
once he resolved to settle down in the pursuit of knowledge, he
moved to Holland "where the long duration of the war has led
to the establishment of such order that the armies maintained
here seem to serve only to make the enjoyment of the fruits of
peace all the more secure" (CSM I 126; AT VI 31). It is not surprising to find him later, then, in the court of Queen Christina,
just after Sweden had won (so to speak) the Thirty Years' War
and had established and was maintaining the peace by force.

E. Constitution of a Swedish Academy of Arts and Sciences
While in the court of Queen Christina, Descartes wrote for her
the constitution of a Swedish Academy of Arts and Sciences.
This is the only statement we have in which Descartes details
how an institution should be organized and directed, and how
its business should be conducted and its conclusions drawn. We
do have hints of this in Descartes's comments cited above in
which he says the opinion and guidance of one man is better
than that of several men. And in other places where he talks

about his own work, he suggests both in the *Discours* (CSM I
151: AT VI 78) and in the *Principia Philosophiae* (CSM I 188; AT
IXB 17) that if people want to help him, they should not come to
work with him, just send money. He certainly indicates his pref-
erence for one-man rule.

I say all this to argue that while it is not surprising to find that
the queen is the head of the academy, that she listens to the
ordered discussion of the members, and that she draws the conclusions, this model is not presented simply because Descartes
is writing for the queen, but also because it expresses his convictions. That is the way he would proceed if he were conduct-
ing an academy, workshop, or laboratory, and there is plenty of
evidence in what I have quoted from the *Discours* that he thinks
that is the way a government should be organized, too. It is, in
fact, theoretically how the monarchy in both Sweden and
France was organized. The only thing missing in Descartes's
writings and in my construction of Descartes's political philosophy is a prime minister. Of course there were prime ministers,
such as Richelieu and Mazarin, acting as the chief decision mak-
ers and holders of power in Descartes's time, and he well knew
it. It was politic of him not to say anything about this when he
wrote of the greatness of monarchs, but, more to the point, he
would certainly not object to rule by a prime minister so long as
it was monolithic.

The second article in Descartes's draft of the constitution for
the Swedish Academy is a specification that only subjects of the
crown can be members. I suspect that Descartes included this
provision because he himself wanted to escape from Sweden
and so ruled himself out as a member of the Academy. But there
is also a suggestion here of a predilection for nationalism that I
include as an aspect of Descartes's political philosophy.

F. *Les Passions de l'Ame*

How does Descartes think a citizen of a state ought to behave?
Les Passions de l'Ame is packed with material that can be used

to construct Descartes's ideal citizen. For my purposes, however, what is most striking is how the third maxim of Descartes's code of conduct, about mastering oneself rather than fortune and changing one's desires rather than the order of the world, so completely prefigures and summarizes the essential message of *Les Passions de l'Ame*. This is that the conquest of the will is the highest attainment of man. (And of course this goes all the way back to Descartes's schooling at La Flèche, where his Jesuit teachers stressed the training of the will.) Descartes says that "the strongest souls belong to those in whom the will by nature can most easily conquer the passions and stop the bodily movements which accompany them" (CSM I 347; AT XI 367). And we can all be strong. Principle 50 is titled "*There is no soul so weak that it cannot, if well-directed, acquire an absolute power over its passions*" (CSM I 248; AT XI 368). Descartes argues (in a passage I have remarked on above) that this has to be the case because we can train dogs not to be gun shy, and

> since we are able, with a little effort, to change the movements of the brain in animals devoid of reason, it is evident that we can do so still more effectively in the case of men. Even those who have the weakest souls could acquire absolute mastery over all their passions if we employed sufficient ingenuity in training and guiding them. (CSM I 348; AT XI 370)

This is, of course, as I indicate above, the physiological foundation of behavior modification and brainwashing. If there is ideological support for brainwashing in Descartes, it would go like this. Everyone does desire to do good. Reason directs one to act for the good, but sometimes bodily desires overcome the desires of reason. We all can, nevertheless, learn to overcome bodily desires. Sometimes, however, this requires the help of friends or the community. But anyone can gain control of his or her passions. Now suppose someone asserts that he or she does not want to overcome bodily desires, and resists learning to control them. A dissident might call this doing one's own thing, or living the natural life, or letting it all hang out. Should this person's friends then take the recalcitrant individual in hand to be reformed willy-nilly? And should the state reform or re-educate dissidents on the ground that they have false consciousnesses and do not know their own good (which, of course, is the good of the state). Certainly if we or the state do know what is best, Descartes doubtless would say that then we have the right to reform lost souls for their own good. Certain knowledge of what is best would support, if necessary, totalitarian measures of behavior modification. I believe, however, that although Descartes would support reform measures for common criminals, he would not support totalitarian behavior control for everyone. He is, after all, tolerant of religions other than his own. He would probably say that with our finite understanding we can never be certain that ultimately we know what is best for everyone. Further, despite Descartes's support of authoritarian monarchy, he is a strong individualist who prizes freedom and who thinks people should improve themselves. This is firmly expressed when he says in *Les Passions de l'Ame* that "we can reasonably be praised or blamed only for actions that depend upon [our] free will" (CSM I 384; AT XI 445). This is the sternly independent Descartes, master of self-control, but also firmly in lockstep with the state. And although he is the ultimate individual in saying that "the fresh satisfaction we gain when we have just performed an action we think good is a passion – a kind of joy which I consider to be the sweetest of all joys, because its cause depends only on ourselves" (CSM I 396; AT XI 471), he also says that the greatest good is not to help oneself but "doing good to others" (CSM I 385; AT I 448).

I go from this to certain ideas in Descartes's political philosophy about education, which might be termed indoctrination. Anyone who reads *Les Passions de l'Ame* cannot help but see that Descartes believes that the ideal man – the ideal citizen – should be in complete, cool control of all his thoughts and passions, and thus in complete control of all his desires and actions. We should control ourselves this way because

> The function of all the passions consists solely in this, that they dispose our soul to want the things that nature deems useful for us, and to persist in this volition; and the same agitation of the spirits that normally causes the passions also disposes the body to make movements that help us to attain these things. (CSM I 349; AT XI 372)

Even love and hate are totally utilitarian: "when we think of something as good with regard to us, i.e., as beneficial to us, this makes us have love for it; and when we think of it as evil or harmful, this arouses hatred in us" (CSM I 350; AT XI 374).

As I show in Chapter 4, Descartes's views on love and hate, and on the conduct of the passions or emotions, are very like those of his contemporary, Pierre Corneille. In Corneille's plays, people consult their reason about whom to love and hate. Then they order their passions or emotions to follow suit.

What this means for education, as Descartes says in the *Discours*, is that because "our will tends to pursue or avoid only what our intellect represents as good or bad, we need only to judge well in order to act well, and to judge as well as we can in order to do our best." He caps this with the claim that "when we are certain of this, we cannot fail to be happy" (CSM I 124; AT VI 28). Descartes believes that this follows from the fact that "our will naturally tends to desire only what our intellect represents to it as somehow possible" (CSM I 124; AT VI 25–26). So, in line with educational theory from the Greeks through Bentham, Mill, and Dewey, Descartes thinks that if people can only be taught to recognize what is good and possible, they will seek to do only the possible and the good.

Thus, Descartes says in *Les Passions de l'Ame* that to gain control, the soul must have "firm and determinate judgments bearing upon the knowledge of good and evil, which the soul has resolved to follow in guiding its conduct," and he goes on to say that

> The weakest souls of all are those whose will is not determined in this way to follow such judgments, but constantly allows itself to be carried away by present passions. The latter, being often opposed to one another, pull the will first to one side and then to the other, . . . and since the will obeys first the one and the other, it is continually opposed to itself, and so it renders the soul enslaved and miserable. (CSM I 347; AT XI 367)

Descartes states explicitly that one of the highest uses of such control of the passions is "in those who have exposed themselves to certain death in defense of their sovereign or their city" (CSM I 358; AT XI 391). So citizens should be taught to control their passions for the defense of the state.

Nevertheless, despite the stress on loyalty to sovereign and state, a strong strain of individualism continues in Descartes from his first publication in 1637, where in a gloss on his first maxim of conduct in the *Discours*, he says that "In particular, I counted as excessive all promises by which we give up some of our freedom" (CSM I 123; AT VI 24) – to his last publication in 1649 where he says in *Les Passions de l'Ame*, "I see only one thing in us that could give us good reason for esteeming ourselves, namely, the exercise of our free will and the control we have over our volitions" (CSM I 384; AT XI 445). Again, there is no excuse for anyone not having perfect control of his will, and "since others have free will just as much as we do, they may use it just as well as we use ours" (CSM I 385; AT XI 447).

Descartes's ideal is the generous man, the gentleman. His description has all the trappings of an ideal self-portrait, so I quote it at length. Descartes says that

> Those who are generous in this way are naturally led to do great deeds, and at the same time not to undertake anything of which they do not feel themselves

capable. And because they esteem nothing more highly than doing good to others and disregarding their own self-interest, they are always perfectly courteous, gracious, and obliging to everyone. Moreover they have complete command over their passions. In particular, they have mastery over their desires, and over jealousy and envy, because everything they think sufficiently valuable to be worth pursuing is such that its acquisition depends only on themselves; over hatred of other people, because they have esteem for everyone; over fear, because of the self-assurance that confidence in their own virtue gives them; and finally over anger, because they have very little esteem for everything that depends on others, and so they never give their enemies any advantage by acknowledging that they are injured by them. (CSM I 385; AT XI 447–448)

Among other things, this passage shows Descartes again insisting on the superiority of the individual, of one man over a committee, in the conduct of any enterprise.

Individualism is supported also by a passage I have quoted above: free will, Descartes says, "renders us in a certain way like God by making us masters of ourselves" (CSM I 384; AT XI 445). And the human being on earth nearest to God is a monarch. But although we are all alike in having this will, Descartes states as an empirical fact that because "there is, it seems, no virtue so dependent on good birth as the virtue that causes us to esteem ourselves in accordance with our true value, . . . it is easy to believe that the souls that God puts into our bodies are not all equally noble and strong" (CSM I 388; AT XI 453). He does go on to offer the consolation to the non-nobly born that "It is certain, however, that a good upbringing is a great help in correcting defects of birth" (CSM I 388; AT XI 453). It is possible, however, for a person to have "a very bad nature" (CSM I 393; AT XI 465).

Descartes shows both his tolerance for different religions in his scorn for bigotry, and also – in his examples – his adherence to monarchy, when he discusses "those who believe themselves devout, but are merely bigoted and superstitious." He goes on to say of bigots that

> These are people who – under the pretext of frequently going to church, reciting many prayers, wearing their hair short, fasting, and giving alms – think they are absolutely perfect and imagine they are such close friends of God that they could not do anything to displease him. They suppose that anything their passion dictates is a commendable zeal, even though it sometimes dictates the greatest crimes that men can commit, such as the betrayal of cities, the killing of sovereigns, and the extermination of whole nations for the sole reason that the citizens do not accept their opinions. (CSM I 396; AT XI 472)

In this passage he also shows his commitment to the community, to monarchy, and to tolerance of others in his listing of "the greatest crimes that man can commit."

Descartes has a consensual, not a contractual, view of society and the state.[2] That is, he asserts that "gratitude . . . is always a virtue and one of the principal bonds of human society" (CSM I 397; AT XI 474). Gratitude derives from being treated according to one's status and deserts, and this fits better with a consensual, than with a contractual, relationship between oneself and God, the sovereign, and the state.

G. Discussion

In *Descartes et l'ordre politique*,[3] Pierre Guenancia argues that Descartes did not write on political philosophy or develop a theory of politics because the human mind and society cannot be explained mechanically, and science, according to Descartes, must be deterministically mechanical. "Descartes did not write on politics because for him the soul and society cannot be explained by a mechanism, and science is only mechanistic. Society is a creation of liberty and not a deduction from nature."[4] For Descartes, the world of matter consists of inter-changeable parts interacting deterministically. We can thus describe the behavior of bodies with general natural laws, and explain and predict their behavior with hypothetico-deductive science. Guenancia argues that on this rationalist, mechanist foundation of the sciences of bodies, Hobbes and Spinoza each develop a deterministic science of man in which human beings are considered as interchangeable members of a body politic. Society itself then is treated as being determined according to natural laws, and is explained and predicted deductively.

This rationalist science of human behavior, of society, and of politics is based on a foundation of a common human nature that assures that all individual human members of the mechanism act alike. While according to Descartes there is a common biological nature, Guenancia argues that the freedom of human will and action precludes any common mental nature that determines the individual personalities of each human being. Because the individuals who act in social interactions and thereby create political institutions such as the state, are free, their behavior is not describable by general natural laws, so there can be no science of human behavior. That is why, Guenancia argues, there is no truly Cartesian social science or political philosophy.

Although Guenancia does not develop a Cartesian political philosophy, he does argue that Cartesian rationalism has had and continues to have an immense impact on the development of individualism and liberal democracy. This is in contrast to the extension of the deterministic tendencies of rationalism that in Hobbes, Spinoza, and Pascal support totalitarian political institutions. In this interpretation, Guenancia follows the lead of Noam Chomsky who argues, most notably in *Cartesian Lingusitics*,[5] that the human mind is not amenable to integration in a deterministic scientific model. Harry M. Bracken, in "Rationalism and Dualism in Descartes" and "Essence, Accident, and Race" in his *Mind and Language*,[6] has carried the discussion of the political implications of Cartesian rationalism even further. Bracken argues that the open nature of the free Cartesian mind is a defense against totalitarianism, in contrast to the Lockean blank-tablet mind of empiricism, which lends itself to molding by totalitarian regimes into whatever sort of member-part the body politic needs. Guenancia follows Chomsky and Bracken in presenting Descartes's resistant and unpredictable free will as a major oppositional force to political totalitarianism.

Guenancia argues that Descartes is conservative in following local customs and laws, not because of reverence for tradition or the wisdom of the ages, but simply because he believes there is no science of politics and thus no best system. Descartes can uncynically and responsibly be a spectator rather than an actor, because he believes the individual has no necessary place in society. In a passage reminiscent of George Orwell, Guenancia says that "the idea of an independent individual opposed to the polity [or state] surely contributes to the modern myth of the omnipresence and omnipotence of selected editing and intimidation."[7] Guenancia finds Descartes opposed not just to the allure of the deterministic mechanism, but even more to the mystique of the holistic organism as a description (and not just a metaphor) of the state as developed by Hobbes, Spinoza, and Pascal.[8]

The most striking contrast Guenancia draws between Descartes and the totally deterministic rationalism that covers both mind and body in Hobbes and Spinoza and that leads Pascal to retreat to religious and mystical irrationalism is the fact that Descartes insists that life is good.[9] What is more, in opposition to the ascetic Christian denial of the passions, Descartes says that a man of the strongest passions can most enjoy life. Far from suggesting that one try to undertake the impossible task of suppressing the passions (which are determined in the mechanistic bodily system), Descartes shows how one can direct them to fulfill one's desires for a good and generous and happy life. Guenancia interprets Descartes not only as an opponent of Hobbesian and Spinozistic holistic totalitarianism, but also as an advocate of an exuberant, individualistic approach to life and society based on generous intentions and a strong free will. Guenancia calls this Cartesian approach to politics *"Exteriorization,"*[10] and compares Descartes's notion of society to Popper's open society.[11]

Someone who does derive totalitarianism, or at least absolute sovereignty, from Descartes's omnipotent God is Karl Th. Buddeberg. In his "Descartes und der politische Absolutismus," he says that "Descartes's philosophy is not the metaphysical origin of the explanation of the rights of man, but of the authority of the absolute sovereign."[12] Just as Descartes's God creates laws of nature and morality, so does the prince have absolute sovereignty over his subjects. Buddeberg thus implies that kings on earth have the power to create civil law to which no subject could or should object. But he admits that Descartes holds that the human understanding is limited, so men sin and err by making judgments beyond their knowledge. Buddeberg does not, however, draw the Cartesian conclusion that kings, too, are men, and so cannot – as God does – establish what is right and true by willing it. And Buddeberg ignores the overwhelming evidence of Descartes's commitment to individualism.

In *L'individualité selon Descartes*, Rodis-Lewis argues that Descartes's philosophy does not support an individualism.[13] I cannot discuss that major thesis here, but I will treat the question from the limited viewpoint of Descartes's political philosophy.

In a letter to Princess Elisabeth of November, 1646, Descartes says he finds nothing bad in Machiavelli's *Discourse on Titus Livius* (AT IV 531). But in another letter to her also of November, 1646, he discusses *The Prince* and carefully separates "princes who have acquired a state by just ways [from] those who have usurped a state by illegitimate means" (AT IV 486). Machiavelli errs in using as an example an illegitimate rather than a legitimate sovereign.

Supposing the prince were legitimate, the major question that arises is whether the moral rules for individuals and individual goals are different from those for sovereigns and states, and, if so, which takes precedence. I agree with Rodis-Lewis,[14] Mesnard,[15] and Lefèvre[16] that Descartes believes with Machiavelli that the rights and goals of individuals are subordinate to those of the sovereign and the state. But the difference between Descartes and Machiavelli is, as Lefèvre says, that Descartes *"always makes political relativity yield to an absolute morality."*[17]

Descartes's absolute morality and his notion of the good stemming from God pertains to individual citizens as much as to the prince, so there can be no real basis for distinguishing between different moral rules and goals for individuals and princes. Mesnard makes this point quite explicit in saying that "the Cartesian hypothesis assumes first a prince who is legitimate and probably a prince who is Christian."[18] In effect, then, Descartes's "Christian Machiavellianism" provides for no transvaluation of values by the prince, but is instead the basis for a monarchy in which the goals of the state are sought equally by both individual citizens and the sovereign. Then for Descartes, as opposed to Machiavelli, the subordination of individuals to the sovereign is based on the natural superiority in wisdom of legitimate princes. But this does not rule out individualism, for Descartes's individual citizen and the sovereign have the same moral principles and goals.

Thus, with the qualification that individuals have the ultimate goals of the state or community in mind, I agree with Guenancia's derivation of extreme individualism from Descartes's principle of free will. But as Guenancia himself says in the last sentence of his book, "But for all this, one must *assume* that we are free."[19] Guenancia does a lot of inferential extrapolation to give a plausible argument why Descartes did not develop a political philosophy. My construction is not as venturesome as Guenancia's, being based more on Descartes's practical actions and his writings than on his metaphysical principle of freedom. As Guenancia does not conceal, a crucial problem in Cartesian metaphysics concerns how human action can be free when the mind is linked with a body that is integrated in a deterministic mechanical system.[20] Descartes does not solve this problem, nor does Guenancia attempt to treat it. I think it is fair, therefore, to develop, at least hypothetically as I do here, a Cartesian political philosophy.

But just how Machiavellian is Descartes's political philosophy? Richard Kennington says that "Descartes asserts that there is a 'law that obliges us to procure so far as it is in us, the general good of all men [AT V 61]...the only categorical obligation ever asserted by Descartes."[21] Kennington notes that this term "'good of men' . . . lacks the sense of community of 'the common good.'"[22] Descartes stresses generosity, and does not mention justice as a virtue nor is he a political egalitarian. "Generous minds, or 'strong and noble minds' have their strength from birth, or by nature, hence are 'masters' by nature, a natural nobility or aristocracy."[23] Through his self-esteem, the generous man works toward the mastery of nature for the good of all men, "and benevolence thus understood becomes the substitute for justice."[24] Kennington argues that this is in fact "a threat to the traditional foundations of society [because] the support of the project of science by the most liberal as well as the most tyrannical regimes in modern times [shows that this form of the] mastery of nature...is relatively neutral to the differences among types of regimes."[25] Thus, "the useful sought by the generous minds is not identical with the useful sought by society."[26] Enlightenment demands reform leading to an open society:

> The common means, the advancement of science, cannot be achieved without a certain transformation,

or new "legislation," of social institutions. Science will advance only if the free exchange of "experiments" or free communication is sanctioned within the borders of society, but also between societies; it will achieve its promise only if society also promotes science by the endowment of scientists with safety, income, and deference. The free exchange cannot be limited to exchange of knowledge: societies, or more precisely, the political authorities, are not competent judges of knowledge. Hence society must not only sanction the competent or the scientists as judges but must sanction all communication of doctrines.[27]

Kennington thus says that "by the promise of the progress of science toward infinite benefits [Descartes] and Bacon established the 'idea of progress' or the belief that the good is the future whose benevolence owes nothing to tradition, to nature, or to God."[28]

Kennington argues in conclusion that these political implications originally stemmed from Machiavelli, that it was "Machiavelli's incipient critique of the impurities of natural reason [that] demanded that nature be remedied, or rather mastered, by art, or by the construction of a method."[29] Thus Kennington remarks on "the amazingly similar statements of the doctrine concerning 'reformation' of political bodies by a private individual in the Prince (chapter vi), the New Organon (Book I, section 129), and the Discours (Part II)."[30] And in this sense I agree that Descartes's political philosophy is not only individualistic and Baconian, but also Machiavellian.

In his *Descartes politico: o della ragionevole ideologia*,[31] Antonio Negri concludes that Descartes does not have a political philosophy, but presents what is basically a rationalist, monarchist, humanist ideology:

Is this not Cartesian science then? Is it not science above all in its opening upon the world of sociality and history? It is not a mirroring of reality, and it is not an analytic reconstruction of a world apart. What then is it? It is a fiction, what we would call today an ideology. It is a rational ideology extended over the space of the crisis of the seventeenth century, that age of lack of faith and of equilibrium, with the hope of reconstruction. What is operating here is a humanistic nostalgia.[32]

The conservatism of Descartes's provisional morality in the *Discours*, according to Negri, is calculated to attain social obedience. Descartes is primarily concerned to attain and maintain peace, "legality . . . against disorder."[33] To this end, Descartes appeals to Machiavelli, although he does not know his works very well. Nevertheless:

There is a great deal of the true Machiavelli in the rational Cartesian ontology! In Descartes as in Machiavelli there is a general sense of the end of the humanistic revolution and the necessity of recasting bourgeois behavior in these new conditions. There is always a movement toward that end.[34]

In the end, then, we have "an 'ambiguous' Descartes, and perhaps this is the best definition of a Descartes 'politico.'"[35] Negri says that Descartes's dualistic philosophy, separating absolutely man from God, man from the world, and God from the world, the free will of man from the mechanistic determinism of the material world, and ultimately man from society – leads to a crisis: "This expresses the most intense moment of crisis between the civil society and the state, the moment of maximum separation and most profound dualism."[36] Negri thinks Descartes is pessimistic about the participation of the bourgeoisie in the improvement of society, but this interpretation is based on Negri's apparent belief that only through faith and God's grace can a "utopian" society be assured.[37]

In the end, Descartes certainly did not believe this, nor was he pessimistic about society. Descartes was optimistic about man's future. To be sure, Cartesian social order rests on the common man's belief in God and a moral order, and on absolutism or royalism, but Descartes was sure that material goodness and the comforts of life will follow man's conquest of nature through the advancement of secular natural science as developed by private individuals like himself. This approach to the good life is both the motivation and the goal of Descartes's political philosophy.[38]

ENDNOTES

Endnotes for Chapter 2

1 Gustave Cohen, *Écrivains français en Hollande dans la première moitié du XVIIe siècle*, Paris: Édouard Champion, 1920, p. 681.

2 Sven Stolpe, *Christina of Sweden*, translated by Alec Randall and Ruth Mary Bethell, London: Burns & Oates, 1966, pp. 115–22.

Endnotes for Chapter 3

1 Adrien Baillet, *La vie de monsieur Des-Cartes*, Paris: Daniel Horthemels, 1691, Vol. 2, p. 395.

2 In her Descartes: biographie (Paris: Calmann-Lévy, 1995, p. 275), Geneviève Rodis-Lewis cites Morhof's 1692 *Polyhistor* as a source independent of Baillet that she says proves that Descartes wrote the ballet. But Morhof was a compiler of references, and he could have concluded that Descartes wrote the ballet after he had seen that attribution in Baillet's life of Descartes published in 1691.

3 Albert Thibaudet and Johan Nordström, "Un ballet de Descartes: La Naissance de la paix," *La revue de Genève*, Vol. 1, 1920, pp. 163–85.

4 [René Descartes (?)], *La Naissance de la paix*, in *Samlade Skrifter av Georg Stiernhielm*, Johan Nordström and Berndt Olsson, eds., Lund: Carl Bloms, 1976, Vol. 3, pp. 303–16.

5 [René Descartes (?)] and Louis Aragon, *La Naissance de la paix*. Paris: Bibliothèque Française, 1946; German translation by Hans Paeschke, *Die Geburt des Friedens*, Neuwied am Rhein: Lancelot Verlag, 1949.

6 Gustave Cohen, "Descartes et le ballet de cour," *La Revue internationale de musique*, Vol. 9, 1950, p. 233.

7 Agne Beijer, "La Naissance de la paix; ballet de cour de René Descartes," in *Le lieu théâtral à la Renaissance*, Jean Jacquot, ed., Paris: Centre National de la Recherche, 1946, p. 410.

8 Ibid., pp. 412–15.

9 William McC. Stewart, "Descartes and Poetry," *The Romanic Review*, Vol. 29, 1938, p. 232.

10 Ibid.

11 Beijer, op. cit., p. 418.

12 *Johan Ekeblads bref*, N. Söberg, ed., Stockholm, 1911, p. 19, quoted in Lars Gustafsson, "Amor et Mars vaincus: allégorie politique des ballets de cour de l'époque de la Reine Christina" in *Queen Christina of Sweden: Documents and Studies*, Magnus von Platen, ed., Nationalmusei Skriftserie nr. 12, Analecta Reginesia 1, Stockholm: P. A. Norstedt & Söner, 1966, p. 87.

13 Baillet, op. cit., pp. 407–8. . . . un petit traité touchant la manière de faire des armes sous le titre de *l'Art d'Escrime*.

14 Stewart, op. cit., p. 233.

15 *Palmsköldiana* 361:675; *cf.* G. E. Klemming, *Sveriges Dramatiska Litteratur til och med 1875, Bibliografi*, Stockholm: P. A. Nordstedt & Söner, 1863–1879, pp. 34–35. Klemming, also, says he doubts that Descartes wrote *La Naissance de la paix*. Klemming surely knew that the ballet is attributed to Poirier in *Palmsköldiana*.

16 Carl Silfverstolpe, "Antoine de Beaulieu," *Samlaren Tidskrift*, Uppsala: Akademiska Boktryckereit, 1889, p. 22.

17 Johan Grönstedt, *Baletter, Idyller, Kostymbaler, Spektakler och Upptåg: Uppförda vid Drotting Christinas Hof, Åren 1638–1654*, Stockholm: Brobergs Bok & Accidens-Tryckerii, 1911, p. 77.

18 Thibaudet and Nordström, op. cit., p. 166.

19 Gustafsson, op. cit., p. 99.

20 *La Naissance de la paix*, Stockholm: Jean Janssonius, 1649, p. 8.

21 Stewart, op. cit., p. 222.

22 Baillet, op. cit., p. 395.

23 Ibid.

24 Sven Delblanc, "Baletten som glorifierade Kristinia" in *Svenska Dagbladet*, June 6, 1985, p. 14(10).

25 Rolf Lindborg, "Filosofen Descartes och Kristinia vasa" in *Svenska Dagbladet*, May 29, 1985, p. 14(10).

26 Beijer, op. cit., p. 409.

27 Gustafsson, op. cit., p. 88.

28 Geneviève Rodis-Lewis, *Descartes: biographie.* Paris: Calmann-Lévy, 1995, p. 275; English translation by Jane Marie Todd, *Descartes: His Life and Works.* Ithaca, N.Y.: Cornell University Press, 1998, p. 199.

29 Gilbert Louise, "Une oeuvre poétique de Descartes, les vers du ballet 'La Naissance de Paix,'" *Mémoires de l'académie nationale des sciences, arts et belles-lettres, de Caen,* Vol. 20, 1982, p. 187.

30 John M. Morris, "Letter commenting on Richard A. Watson's note and translation 'Descartes's Ballet?'" in *American Philosophical Association Proceedings,* Vol. 63, No. 1, 1989, pp. 10–12, *American Philosophical Association Proceedings,* Vol. 63, No. 5, p. 61.

31 Louise, op. cit., p. 189.

32 Ibid, p. 191.

33 Gustafsson, op. cit., p. 97.

34 Dimitri Davidenko, *Descartes le scandaleux,* Paris: Robert Laffont, 1988. See also Alexandre Astruc, *Le Roman de Descartes,* Paris: Ballard, 1989, on the cover of which it says, "It is a Descartes not like the others who is depicted here, a Descartes cavalier of the impossible, brother of d'Artagnan, of the Cid of Corneille, a Descartes who makes his way with the point of his sword and who is at the same time an experimenter, a jack-of-all-trades of genius, who shares in the conquest of a new world." More realistic, but still romanticized, is the Descartes of Brigette Hermann, *Histoire de mon esprit ou le roman de la vie de René Descartes,* Paris: Bartillat, 1996.

35 This comes through in Irene Behn's *Der Philosoph und die Königin: Renatus Descartes und Christina Wasa, Briefwechsel und Begegnung,* Freiburg/München: Karl Alber, 1957, despite all the sweetness and light in this charming rendition of the story.

36 Frédéric Lachèvre, "Hélie Poirier," *Glanes bibliographiques et littéraires,* Paris: L. Giraud-Badin, 1929, Vol. 2, pp. 124–37.

37 Ibid., p. 128.

38 Ibid., pp. 130–31.

39 H. W. Van Tricht, "Hélie Poirier, Translator of Erasmus," *Quaerendo,* Vol. 10, 1980, p. 153.

40 Box No. 10, 3N ms. fr. 3970. 128 & 130, Carolina Rediviva. Bibliothèque Nationale, Manuscrits français 3930.

41 Henri de Brasset, *Registre des lettres et des despaches que j'ay escrittes en l'année 1649 durant ma Residence en Holland.* From de Brasset à de la Thuillierie de 9 December 1649, BN.fr.17901, f857v.

Endnotes for Chapter 5

1 Gustave Lanson, "Le héros cornélien et le 'généreux' selon Descartes," *Revue d'histoire littéraire de la France*, Vol. I, 1894, p. 397.

2 Ibid., p. 398.

3 Ibid., p. 401.

4 Ibid., p. 403.

5 Ibid., p. 410.

6 Ibid.

7 Ibid., pp. 410–11.

8 Ernst Cassirer, *Descartes, Corneille, Christine de Suède*, translated by Madeline Francès and Paul Schrecker, Paris: J. Vrin, 1941, p. 9.

9 Ibid.

10 Ibid., pp. 12–13.

11 Ibid., p. 18.

12 Ibid., p. 26.

13 Ibid.

14 Ibid., p. 31.

15 Ibid., p. 37.

16 Cornelia Serrurier, "Saint François de Sales – Descartes – Corneille," *Neophilologus*, Vol. 3, 1918, pp. 89–99.

17 Ibid., p. 89,

18 Ibid., p. 96.

19 Ibid., p. 98.

20 Robert Champigny, "Corneille et le *Traité des passions*," *The French Review*, Vol. 26, 1952, pp. 112–20.

21 Ibid., p. 112.

22 Ibid., p. 113.

23 Ibid., p. 117.

24 Ibid., p. 120.

25 William McC. Stewart, "Descartes and Poetry," *The Romanic Review*, vol. 29, 1938, p. 213.

26 Ibid.

27 Ibid., p. 214.

28 Ibid., p. 216.

29 Ibid., pp. 218–19.

30 Ibid., p. 219.

31 Ibid., p. 224.

32 Jean-Marie Beyssade, "Descartes et Corneille ou les démesures de l'égo," *Laval théologique et philosophique*, Vol. 47, 1991, pp. 63–82.

Endnotes for Chapter 6

1 In this I agree with Rainer Specht, "Über Descartes' Politische Ansichten," *Der Staat*, Vol. 3, 1964, pp. 281–94; Roman Schnur, *Individualismus und Absolutismus: Zur politischen Theorie vor Thomas Hobbes (1600–1640)*, Berlin: Dunker & Humbolt, 1963, pp. 74–75; and Carl Schmitt, "Der Staat als Mechanismus bei Hobbes und Descartes," *Dem Gedächtnis an René Descartes (300 Jahr Discours de la Méthode)* (zugleich Band 30 Heft 4 des *Archivs für Rechts- und Sozialphilosophie*), ed. C. A. Emge, Berlin: Verlag für Staatswissenschaften und Geschichte, 1937, pp. 158–68.

2 I agree with Specht that, as opposed to Hobbes, Descartes does not have a contract theory.

3 Pierre Guenancia, *Descartes et l'ordre politique*, Paris: Presses Universitaires de France, 1979.

4 Ibid., p. 97.

5 Noam Chomsky, *Cartesian Linguistics: A Chapter in the History of Rationalist Thought*, New York: Harper & Row, 1966.

6 Bracken, *Mind and Language: Essays on Descartes and Chomsky*, Dordrecht: Foris, 1983, pp. 1–38, 39–50.

7 Guenancia, op. cit., p. 199, passim.

8 Ibid., p. 226.

9 Ibid., p. 219.

10 Ibid., p. 101.

11 Ibid., p. 231.

12 Karl Th. Buddeberg, "Descartes und der politische Absolutismus," in C. A. Emge, ed., *Dem Gedächtnis an René Descartes (300 Jahr Discours de la Méthode)* (zugleich Band 30 Heft 4 des *Archivs für Rechts- und Sozialphilosophie*), Berlin, Verlag für Staatswissenschaften und Geschichte, 1937, p. 94.

13 Geneviève Lewis [Rodis-Lewis], *L'individualité selon Descartes*, Paris: J. Vrin, 1950.

14 Geneviève Rodis-Lewis, *La morale de Descartes*, Paris: Presses Universitaires de France, 1970, pp. 104–9.

15 Pierre Mesnard, *Essai sur la morale de Descartes*, Paris: Boivin, 1936, pp. 190–212.

16 Roger Lefèvre, *L'humanisme de Descartes*, Paris: Presses Universitaires de France, 1957, pp. 154–55.

17 Ibid., p. 152.

18 Mesnard, op. cit., p. 209.

19 Guernancia, op. cit., p. 255, his italics.

20 Richard A. Watson, "What Moves the Mind? An Excursion in Cartesian Dualism," in *The Breakdown of Cartesian Metaphysics*, Boston: Hackett, 1998, pp. 181–92.

21 Richard Kennington, "René Descartes 1596–1650" in Leo Strauss and Joseph Cropsey, eds. *History of Political Philosophy*, Chicago: Rand McNally, 1963, p. 386.

22 Ibid., p. 387.

23 Ibid., p. 390.

24 Ibid., p. 391.

25 Ibid.

26 Ibid.

27 Ibid., pp. 391–92.

28 Ibid., p. 394.

29 Ibid.

30 Ibid.

31 Antonio Negri, *Descartes politico: o della ragionevole ideologia*, Milano: Feltrinelli Editore, 1970.

32 Ibid., p. 157.

33 Ibid., p. 115.

34 Ibid., p. 165.

35 Ibid., p. 209.

36 Ibid., p. 119.

37 Ibid., pp. 114–26.

38 In a discussion on the question of whether or not Descartes himself had or presented a Cartesian political theory, Jean-Marie Beyssade, Théo Verbeek, Blandine Barret-Kriegel, and Geneviève Rodis-Lewis conclude that although Descartes recognizes and even appeals to some political principles, particularly those of monarchy, he never explicitly proposes a theory of politics.

BIBLIOGRAPHY

Adam, Charles. *Descartes: sa vie et ses oeuvres: étude historique.* Vol. 12 of Oeuvres de Descartes, edited by Charles Adam and Paul Tannery. Paris: Léopold Cerf, 1910.

Adam, Charles. *Descartes: ses amitiés féminines.* Paris: Boivin, 1937.

Baillet, Adrien. *La vie de monsieur Des-Cartes.* 2 vols. Paris: D. Horthemels, 1691. Reprinted, 2 vols. New York: Garland, 1987.

Barret-Kriegel, Blandine. "Politique-(s) de Descartes?" *Archives de philosophie*, Vol. 53, 1990, pp. 371–88.

Behn, Irene. *Der Philosoph und die Königin: Renatus Descartes und Christina Wasa, Briefwechsel und Begegnung.* Freiburg/München: Karl Alber, 1957.

Beijer, Agne. "La Naissance de la paix: ballet de cour de René Descartes." In *Le lieu théâtral à la renaissance*, edited by Jean Jacquot. Paris: Centre National de la Recherche Scientifique, 1964, pp. 409–22.

Beys de, Charles. *La Pompe de la felicité.* Stockholm: Jean Janssonius, 1650.

[Beys de, Charles.] *Parnasse triomphant.* Stockholm: Jean Janssonius, 1651.

Beyssade, Jean-Marie. "Descartes et Corneille ou les démesures de l'égo." *Laval théologique et philosophique*, Vol. 47, 1991, pp. 63–82.

Beyssade, Jean-Marie. "Présentation," *Archives de philosophie*, Vol. 53, 1990, pp. 353–56.

Biegel, Heidi. "La Naissance de la Paix: A Ballet by René Descartes." Department of Dance, University of California, Los Angeles. Manuscript, 21 pp.

Blom, John J. *Descartes: His Moral Philosophy and Psychology.* New York: New York University Press, 1975. [Contains English translations of Descartes's correspondance with Pollot, Elisabeth, Chanut, and Christina.]

Bracken, Harry M. *Mind and Language: Essays on Descartes and Chomsky.* Dordrecht: Foris, 1984.

Buddeberg, Karl Th. "Descartes und der politische Absolutismus," *Dem Gedächtnis an René Descartes (300 Jahr Discours de la Méthode)* (zugleich Band 30 Heft 4 des *Achives für Rechts- und Sozialphilosophie*), ed. C. A. Emge, Berlin: Verlag für Staatswissenschaften und Geschichte, 1937, pp. 77–96.

Cassirer, Ernst. *Descartes, Corneille, Christine de Suède.* Translated by Madeleine Francès and Paul Schrecker. Paris: J. Vrin, 1942.

Champigny, Roger. "Corneille et le Traité des passions." *The French Review*, Vol. 26, 1952–1953, pp. 112–20.

Chappel, Vere and Willis Doney, eds. *Twenty-Five Years of Descartes Scholarship, 1960–1984: A Bibliography.* New York: Garland, 1987.

Cohen, Gustave. Descartes et le ballet de cour. *La Revue internationale de musique.* Vol. 9, 1950, pp. 233–37.

Cohen, Gustave. *Écrivains français en Hollande dans la première moitié du 17e siècle.* Paris: Édouard Champion, 1920.

Davidenko, Dimitri. *Descartes le scandaleux.* Paris: Robert Laffont, 1988. [Presented as a historical study, this work would be better classified as a novel.]

Brasset, Henri de. *Registre des lettres et des despaches en j'ay escrittes en l'année 1649 durant ma Residence en Holland.* Bibliothèque Nationale, BN.fr.17901.

Delblanc, Sven. "Baletten som glorifierade Kristina." *Svenska Dagbladet*, 6 June 1985, p. 14(10).

Descartes, René. *Compendium of Music.* Translated by Walter Robert. N.P.: American Institute of Musicology, 1961.

[Descartes, René(?).] *La Naissance de la paix.* Stockholm: Jean Janssonius, 1649; German translation by Johannes Freinsheimius, *Des Friedens Geburts-tag*, Stockholm, Heinrich Keysern, 1649; Swedish version by Georg Stiernhielm, *Freds-Afl*, Stockholm: Heinrich Keysern, 1649.

[Descartes, René(?).] *La Naissance de la paix.* In *Samlade Skrifter av Georg Stiernhielm*, edited by Johan Nordstrom and Berndt Olsson, Lund: Carl Bloms, 1976, Vol. VIII, pp. 303–16; German translation by Johannes Freinsheimius, *Des Friedens Geburts-tag*, ibid., pp. 316–29; Swedish version by Georg Stiernhielm, *Freds-Afl, Samlade Skrifter av Georg Stiernhielm*, edited by Johan Nordström, Bernt Olsson, and Per Wieselgren, Lund: Carl Bloms, 1973, Vol. VIII, pp. 81–99.

Descartes, René. *Oeuvres de Descartes.* Edited by Charles Adam and Paul Tannery, nouvelle édition en co-édition avec le Centre National de la Recherche Scientifique, various editors for 11 volumes, Paris, J. Vrin, 1964–1974.

Descartes, René. *The Philosophical Writings of Descartes.* Translated by John Cottingham, Robert Stoothoff, and Dugald Murdoch. 2 volumes. Cambridge: Cambridge University Press, 1985.

[Descartes, René(?) and] Louis Aragon. *La Naissance de la paix.* Paris: Bibliothèque Française, 1946; German translation by Hans Paeschke, *Die Geburt des Friedens*, Neuwied am Rhein: Lancelot Verlag, 1949.

Dimier, Louis. *La vie raisonnable de Descartes.* Paris: Plon, 1926.

Gilson, Henri. *La liberté chez Descartes et la théologie*. Paris: Félix Alcan, 1913.

Grönstedt, Johan. *Svenska Hoffester: Baletter, Idyller, Kostymbaler, Spektakler och Upptåg: Uppförda vid Drottning Christinas Hof, Åren 1638–1654*. Stockholm: Brobergs Bok & Accidens-Tryckeri, 1911.

Guenancia, Pierre. *Descartes selon l'order politique*. Paris: Presses Universitaires de France, 1983.

Gueroult, Martial. *Descartes selon l'ordre des raisons*. 2 vols. Paris: Augier, 1953. English translation by Roger Ariew, 2 vols. *Descartes' Philosophy Interpreted according to the Order of Reasons*. Minneapolis: University of Minnesota Press, 1984, 1985.

Gustafsson, Lars. "Amor et Mars vaincus: allégorie politique des ballets de cour de l'époque de la Reine Christine." In *Queen Christina of Sweden: Documents and Studies*. Edited by Magnus von Platen. Nationalmusei skriftserie nr. 12, Analecta Reginesia 1. Stockholm: P. A. Norstedt & Söner, 1966, pp. 87–99.

Kennington, Richard. "René Descartes 1596–1650." In *History of Political Philosophy*. Edited by Leo Strauss and Joseph Cropsey. Chicago. Rand McNally, 1963, pp. 370–96.

Kenny, Anthony. *Descartes: A Study of His Philosophy*. New York: Random House, 1968.

Klemming, G. E. *Sveriges Dramtiska Litteratur til och med 1875, Bibliografi*. Stockholm: F. A. Norestedt & Söner, 1863–1879.

Lachèvre, Frédéric. "Hélie Poirier," *Glanes bibliographiques et littéraires*, Paris: L. Giraud-Badin, 1929, Vol. 2, pp. 124–37.

Lanson, Gustave. "Le Héros cornélien et le 'généreux' selon Descartes." *Revue d'Histoire littéraire de la France*. Vol. I, 1894, pp. 397–411.

Lefèvre, Roger. *L'humanisme de Descartes*. Paris: Presses Universitaires de France, 1957.

Leroy, Maxime. *Descartes: le philosophe au masque.* 2 vols. Paris: Rieder, 1929.

Leroy, Maxime. *Descartes Social.* Paris: J. Vrin, 1931.

Lewis [Rodis-Lewis], Geneviève. *L'individualité selon Descartes.* Paris: J. Vrin, 1950.

Lindborg, Rolf. "Filosofen Descartes och Kristina vasa." *Svenska Dagbladet,* May 29, 1985, p. 14(10).

Louise, Gilbert. "Une oeuvre poétique de Descartes, les vers du ballet 'La Naissance de la paix,'" *Mémoires de l'académie nationale des sciences, arts et belles-lettres, de Caen,* Vol. 20, 1982, pp. 175–203.

Marshall, John. *Descartes's Moral Theory.* Ithaca, N.Y., and London: Cornell University Press, 1998.

Mesnard, Pierre. *Essai sur la morale de Descartes.* Paris: Boivin, 1935.

Morhofii, Danielis Georgia. *Polyhistor,* ed. 4ª, t. II. Lubecae: Petri Beeckmanni, 1747.

Morris, John M. "Letter commenting on Richard A. Watson's note and translation 'Descartes's Ballet?'" *American Philosophical Association Proceedings,* Vol. 63, No. 5, p. 61.

Negri, Antonio. *Descartes politico: o della ragionevole ideologia.* Milano: Feltrinelli Editore, 1970.

Palmsköldiana. Manuscript 361:675, Carolina Rediviva, Uppsala Universitetsbibliotek, 1724.

Petit, Léon. *Descartes et la Princesse Elisabeth: roman d'amour vécu.* Paris: A.-G. Nizet, 1969. [Despite the subtitle, this is not a novel, but an historical study.]

Pirro, André. *Descartes et la musique.* Paris: Feschbacher, 1907.

Poirier, Hélie. "Letters to Saumaise." In the Johan Nordström collection in the Carolina Rediviva, Box No. 10, 3N ms. fr. 3970. 128 & 130.

Poirier, Hélie. *La Diane Victorieuse.* Stockholm: Jan Janssonius,

1649; also printed as *Le Vaincu de Diane*. Stockholm: Jan Janssonius, 1649.

[Poirier, Hélie.] *Les Passions Victorieuses et Vaincues.* Stockholm: Jan Janssonius, 1649.

Poirier, Hélie. *Le Vaincu de Diane.* Stockholm: Jan Janssonius, 1649; also printed as *La Diane Victorieuse.* Stockholm: Jan Janssonius, 1649.

Rodis-Lewis, Geneviève. *See also* Geneviève Lewis.

Rodis-Lewis, Geneviève. *Descartes: biographie.* Paris: Calmann-Lévy, 1995; English translation by Jane Marie Todd, *Descartes: His Life and Works.* Ithaca, N.Y.: Cornell University Press, 1998.

Rodis-Lewis, Geneviève. "Liberté et égalité chez Descartes," *Archives de philosophie*, Vol. 53, 1990, pp. 421–30.

Rodis-Lewis, Geneviève. *La morale de Descartes.* Paris: Presses Universitaires de France, 1970.

Schmitt, Carl. "Der Staat als Mechanismus bei Hobbes und Descartes." In *Dem Gedächtnis an René Descartes (300 Jahr Discours de la Méthode)* (zugleich Band 30 Heft 4 des *Archivs für Rechts- und Sozialphilosophie*), ed. C. A. Emge, Berlin: Verlag für Staatswissenschaften und Geschichte, 1937, pp. 158–68.

Schnur, Roman. *Individualismus und Absolutismus: Zur politischen Theorie vor Thomas Hobbes (1600–1640).* Berlin: Dunker & Humbolt, 1963.

Sebba, Gregor. *Bibliographia Cartesiana: A Critical Guide to the Descartes Literature: 1800–1960.* International Archives of the History of Ideas 5. The Hague: Martinus Nijhoff, 1964.

Serrurier, Cornelia. *Descartes: l'homme et le penseur.* Paris: Presses Universitaires de France, 1951.

Serrurier, Cornelia. "Saint François de Sales – Descartes – Corneille." *Neophilologus*, Vol. 3, 1918, pp. 89–99.

Silfverstolpe, Carl. "Antoine de Beaulieu." *Samlaren Tidskrift.* Upsala: Akademiska Boktryckerieeit, 1889, pp. 5–30.

Specht, Rainer. "Über Descartes' Politische Ansichten." *Der Staat: Zeitschrift für Staatslehre*, Vol. 3, 1964, pp. 281–94

Stiernhielm, Georg. *Samlade Skrifter*, Johan Nordstrom and Bernt Olsson, editors, Volume 8, Poetiska Skrifter, Lund: Carl Bloms, 1976.

Stewart, William McC. "Descartes and Poetry." *The Romanic Review.* Vol. 29, 1938, pp. 212–42.

Stolpe, Sven. *Christina of Sweden.* Translated by Alec Randal and Ruth Mary Bethell. London: Burns & Oates, 1966.

Thibaudet, Albert and Johan Nordström. "Un ballet de Descartes: La Naissance de la paix." *La Revue de Genève.* Vol. 1, 1920, pp. 163–85.

Van Tricht, H. W. "Hélie Poirier, Translator of Erasmus," *Quaerendo*, Vol. 10, 1980, pp. 153–55.

Verbeek, Théo, "Le contexte néerlandais de la politique cartésienne," *Archives de philosophie*, Vol. 53, 1990, pp. 357–70.

Watson, Richard A. *The Breakdown of Cartesian Metaphysics* Boston: Hackett, 1998.

Watson, Richard A. *Cogito Ergo Sum: The Life of René Descartes.* Boston: David R. Godine, 2002.

Watson, Richard A. "Descartes and Cartesianism," *Encyclopaedia Britannica*, 15th edition, Chicago: Encyclopaedia Britannica, 1989, Vol. 15, pp. 588–95.

Watson, Richard A. "Descartes's Ballet?" *American Philosophical Association Proceedings*, Vol. 63, No. 1, 1989, pp. 10–12.

Watson, Richard A. "René Descartes n'est pas l'auteur de 'La Naissance de la paix'," *Archives de philosophie*, Vol. 53, 1990, pp. 389–401.

Watson, Richard A. "What Moves the Mind? An Excursion in Cartesian Dualism." In *The Breakdown of Cartesian Metaphysics*. Boston: Hackett, 1998, pp.181–92.

INDEX

Abdication of Queen
　　Christina, 29, 51, 55
Adam, Charles, ix, 41, 85
Agony and ecstasy, 71
Amadis de Gaul, 83
Anarchy, 88
Animal spirits, 63
Animal trainers, 73
Aragon, Louis, 42, 115
Astrue. Alexandre, 117
Ausonius, 82–83
L'Art d'Escrime, 46

Bacon, Francis, 112
Baillet, Adrien, viii, 39, 41,
　　45–46, 49–51, 54, 115–16
Balzac, Guez de, 82, 84
Battle of White Mountain, 54
Barret-Kriegel, Blandine, 120
Beaulieu, Antoine de, Ballet
　　Master, 43, 57–58
Behn, Irene, 117
Beijer, Agne, 42, 50, 116–17
Bentham, Jeremy, 103
Beyes, Charles de, 47–49, 54

Beyssade, Jean-Marie, X, 85,
　　119–20
Bodily passions and desires,
　　30, 32, 60, 62–67, 72, 74,
　　100–106
Boethius, 40
Bracken, Harry M., 108, 119
Brainwashing, 73
Brasset, Henri de, 57–58, 118
Brégy, Viscount, M. de
　　Flessel de, vii, 44–45, 53
Brunati, Antonio, 42
Buddeberg, Karl, Th., 109, 119
Bussy, Roger de Rabutin de,
　　77

Calvin, Jean, 81
Cassirer, Ernst, 78–80, 118
Champigny, Robert. 81–82,
　　118
Chanut, Pierre, 37–38, 92
Châtellerault, 91
Chivalry, 83
Chomsky, Noam, 107–8, 119
Cinna, 76

Cleanthes, 40
Clerselier, Claude, 37, 46
Code of conduct, 86, 92–98
Cohen, Gustav, 115
Comedy, 45–46
Comments on a Certain
    Broadsheet, 97
Commerce and industry, 90
Communalism, 99, 106
Conservatism, 93, 95, 113
Costabel, Pierre, ix, 41
Control of nature, 77, 90, 98
Corpus Poetarum, 82
Court ballets, 28, 43
Cropsey, Joseph, 120
Custom and example, 98

Davidenko, Dimitri, 55, 117
Delblanc, Sven, 50, 116
Democracy, 87, 107
Des Friedens Geburts-tag, 43
Despotism, 90
Dewey, John, 103
Discours de la méthode, 34, 66,
    75, 83, 92–99
Dögen, Mathias, 57
Don Sanche d'Aragon, 84
Duben, Andreas, Master of
    the Queen's Music, 43

Edict of Nantes, 91
Educational theory, 103
Ekebald, Johan, 44, 116
Elisabeth, Princess of Bohemia,
    34, 38, 75, 85, 91, 109
Elzevier, Louis, 75, 84–85

Empedocles, 40
Epicurus, 40
Erasmus, Desiderius, 117

Faith of king and nurse, 92
Flemming, Admiral, 38
Frédéric Henri, Prince of
    Orange, 56
Freds-Afl., 43
Freinsheimius, Johannes, 40,
    49–51, 54

Galileo Galilée, 55
Gardie, Count Magnus
    Gabriel de la, 42
Generous man – gentleman,
    104–5
Glory, 31, 32
God, 36, 59, 61, 66–67, 71, 79,
    87, 93, 106, 112–14
Grönstedt, Johan, 116, 117
Guenancia, Pierre, 106–8,
    111, 119–20
Gustafsson, Lars of Örebro,
    51, 54, 116–17

Henry le Grand, 55
Hermann, Brigette, 117
Hobbes, Thomas, 107–9, 119
Horace, 82
Hötton, Godfroy, 56
Humanitarianism, 98, 99
Huygens, Constantin, vi, 46,
    84–85

Individualism, 87, 104–5, 107,
    109–10

Janssonius, Jean, 41–42, 48, 81
Jesuits, 80–81, 101
Jews, 88

Karl Gustav, 29, 55
Kennington, Richard. 111–12, 120
Klemming, G. E., 116

La Haye, 91
La Flèche, 55, 80, 91, 101
La Médée, 75
La Recherche de la Vérité par la Lumière Naturelle, 83
La Rochelle, 54
La Pompe de la Felicité, 47
Lachèvre, Frédéric, 56, 117
Lanson, Gustave, 75–78, 118
Law and lawyers, 33, 84, 90–91
Le Cid, 75
Le Menteur, 84
Le Vaincu de Diane/La Diane Victorieuse, 43–44, 47–48, 51, 54, 57
Leibniz, Gottfried Wilhelm, 46, 83–84
Les Méditations Métaphysiques, 59–60, 75, 97
Les Passions de l'Âme, 38, 60, 72, 77–78, 81, 86, 100–106
Les Passions Victorieuses et Vaincues, 42, 47–48, 51, 54
Letter to Voetius, 36
Lefèvre, Roger, 110, 120

Lewis, Geneviève [Geneviève Rodis-Lewis], 120
Lindborg, Rolf, 50, 116
Louise, Gilbert, 52–53, 117
Love and hate, 37, 54, 103
Lucretius, 40

Machiavelli, Niccolò, 109–10, 112–13
Man in the mask, 82
Maurice, Prince of Nassau, 91
Mazarin, Jules, 100
Mesnard, Pierre, 110, 120
Mill, John Stuart, 103
Moderation, 93
Modern armies, 33
Monarchy, 28, 30, 36, 87, 95, 98, 106, 110
Morhof, Daniel Georg, 40–41, 49–50, 115
Morhof's *Polyhistor*, 40–41, 49–50, 115
Morris, John M., 52–53, 117

Negri, Antonio, 112–14, 120
Nobility, 88–90
Nonhuman animals, 69, 72
Nordström, Johan, 41, 57, 115–16

Olsson, Berndt, 115
Open society, 111–12
Oxenstern, Axel, 56

Paeschke, Hans, 115
Palmsköldiana collection, 48, 51
Pantomime, 43

Parnasse Triomphant, 47
Passions, 30, 32–33, 60–73,
    77–81, 100–106, 108
Pascal, Blaise, 73, 107–8, 119
Peace, 88–90
Peace of Münster, 39, 46
Peace of Westphalia, viii, 34,
    41–42, 53
Pensions for Descartes,
    28–29, 55
Phobias, 66
Picot, Abbé Claude, 37
Pineal gland, 60, 63–65, 67,
    70, 72, 74
Poirier, Hélie, viii, 47–49,
    51–52, 54–58, 116–17
Polyeucte, 76
Pomerania, 28–29
Popkin, Richard H., x
Popper, Karl, 109
Prime minister, 100
Principia Philosophiae, 37, 75,
    100
Protestants, 28, 88, 91–92

Reason, 33, 54, 69–71, 73, 77,
    79–81, 94–95, 97, 100–106
Retz, Jean-François-Paul de
    Gondi de, 77, 80
Republic of the Netherlands,
    28, 55–56, 75, 92
Revolution, 88, 96
Richelieu, Armand Jean du
    Plessis de, 77, 80, 100
Rodis-Lewis, Geneviève, 51,
    109, 115, 117, 120

Rodogune, 76
Saint-Amand, 49
Sales, Saint François de,
    80–81
Scarron, 49
Science and technology, 29,
    90
Schmitt, Carl, 119
Schnur, Roman, 119
School of Arts and Crafts, 86
Schools, 89
Serrurier, Cornelia, 80–81,
    118
Silfverstolpe, Carl, 48, 116
Skepticism, 97
Söberg, N., 115
Socrates, VI, 47
Sophie, Princess of Bohemia,
    85
Soul, 32, 61–63, 68–69, 71–73,
    77, 100–107
Sparta, 95
Spinoza, Baruch, 107–9, 119
State church, 88
Stewart, William McC., 50,
    62, 83, 116, 118
Stiernhielm, Georg, 41, 50–51
Stoicism, 79–80
Stolpe, Sven, 115
Strauss, Leo, 120
Superman, 60
Swedish Academy of Science,
    39, 86, 99–100

Tannery, Paul, ix, 41
Thales, 40

Theater, 82–83

Thibaudet, Albert, 41, 49, 115–16

Thirty Years' War, viii, 29, 33, 42, 99

Thuillerie, Gaspard Coignet de la, 31, 57, 118

Tolerance, 106

Totalitarianism, 73, 87, 102, 107–9

Turenne, Henri de, 77

Van Tricht, H. W., 57, 117

Verbeek, Théo, 120

Viau, Théophile de, 49

Von Specht, Rainer, 119

Varro, 40

Voetius, Gisburtus, 36

War, 88

Watson, Richard A., 117, 120

Weather observations, 38

Welfare of mankind, 98

Women, 34, 79, 89

Xenophanes, 40